What Made Korea Become a Christian Country?

By Takahiro Suzuki

Translated by:

Allen Williams and Sulseob Jo

Copyright 2013 All Rights Reserved Worldwide

Published by

PowerMeUpPublishing

PowerMeUpPublishing.com

ISBN-13: 978-4907477011
ISBN-10: 4907477015

Note from the translators:

This text originally was published in Japanese and translated into English. It contains both Korean and Japanese characters at times within the notes to help reduce ambiguity caused by the inconsistent way that Korean is Romanized. Where it is clearly known, the 'standard' English spellings have been used. The translation was done attempting to capture the meaning and essence of what the author intended and not trying to simply translate word for word. Having a background and knowledge in Japanese, Korean, and English, we feel confident in the translations and spellings, and yet where possible or where confusion existed while translating, the author was asked to clarify and check all translation to make sure that his original intentions were being translated. There are some expressions in Japanese that were used that have been replaced with the best substitutions in English rather than translating the exact Japanese. This was done in order to make the text more accessible to English readers. That said, the English expressions and idioms that were used are from American English. We have done our best to give what we think is the best representation of what Pastor Suzuki wrote in his original Japanese version of this text. If there are still some things that appear unclear, we are the ones to hold accountable.

CONTENTS

Chapter 1 – The Country of Bright Morning

Section 1 The Gentlemen's country of the East

This is the story of the neighboring country of Japan. This story takes place on a small peninsula of East Asia on the far Eastern edge of the Eurasian region. This story is about a people experiencing a new dawn under a clear sky after the blood of many people had been shed.

This peninsula was called JoSeon – (조선 朝鮮 : new dawn) and it was the beginning of them living as one race for a long, long time. They neighbored China at the Amnok River (압록강 鴨緑江), and they continued their tradition and culture. The king of the JoSeon peninsula didn't call himself emperor because the meaning of the title of Emperor is to be the ruler of a large country. They learned this clever way of preserving their country by submission and treating China as a big country. The people in the JoSeon peninsula have stronger emotional connections to China than Japan.

JoSeon people were all using the same language, but the upper class were learning Chinese written characters (한자 漢字) and were reading the characters with Korean pronunciation and using it as their own in their daily lives. In this country in olden times, they were using Chinese characters for writing instead of Korean characters for official documents.

From 1392 till 1910, this peninsula was ruled by the Yi Family, a period of 519 years which is called the JoSeon Dynasty (조선왕조 朝鮮王朝). You can feel how long it is when you think it started at the Muromachi Period (室町時代 : 1336-1573) and continued through the Meiji Period (明治時代 : 1868-1912) in Japan. The JoSeon Dynasty ruled the country by the rules of Confucianism. They had relationships with China, Japan, and Manchuria, nations who shared a similar culture, but were never completely open or deeply involved. The JoSeon people still basically maintained a state of isolationism. They maintained their own separate society through Confucianism.

In the 1800's, European countries such as England and France were colonizing many countries in Asia and Africa. Under this fearful movement the JoSeon Dynasty maintained the policy of isolationism because they remained on the outer edge of Eurasian land. The weak point of this country was that they didn't import any knowledge or skills of weaponry that had progressed so much in Western society.

In 1875, the Japanese battleship Unyogo (雲揚号) attacked Korea on the western coast of the peninsula near Seoul and ordered the country to be opened to outsiders. The difference of firepower between the advanced Japanese army and the Korean army was too great. This is because in 1543 Japan imported western firepower through Tanega Island (種子島) and continued to develop their knowledge and skill of weapon making. Moreover, in the last days of the Tokugawa Shogunate to the Meiji Era, Japan imported new guns and firebombs and battleships from France, England, America, Germany and other places and produced their own weapons based on studying the ones they had imported. In 1894, the Sino-Japanese War found Japan able to stand on equal ground in battle because of the production of the Japanese gun Murata. (Murata Tsuneyosi 村田経芳, 1838-1921, was an inventor and soldier who invented modern guns for Japan.)

Military power at that time meant the quality and methodology of guns and bombs. The JoSeon Dynasty had only weaker firepower because they had kept a closed country policy. The difference between the Tokugawa Shogunate and the JoSeon Dynasty was that the Tokugawa Shogunate held only a half-closed policy to outsiders while the JoSeon Dynasty was fully closed, and that caused the difference in imported weapons and the development of their weapon making ability.

The next year after Unyogo attacked, 1876, the JoSeon Dynasty opened their country. The things that entered at the opening were not only foreign people and trade goods but also the Protestant theology of Christianity. The story of this book is mainly focused on the beginnings and development of this theology in Korea. Without consideration of Christianity, it is impossible to fully understand modern Korean society.

Twenty eight years after Korea becoming an open country, Japan concluded a treaty with the JoSeon Dynasty which permitted the Japanese army to be stationed on the Korean peninsula and established military headquarters in the capitol city of Seoul. Three years after that, in 1907, the Japanese Army succeeded in dismantling the JoSeon Dynasty's army and placed the JoSeon Dynasty under the rule of the Japanese Meiji government. Three more years later, in 1910, the JoSeon Dynasty collapsed and the peninsula was colonized by Japan. It was barely 34 years after the attack of the Unyogo Battleship.

The Change from a Buddhist country to a Confucianism country

Buddhism entered the Korean peninsula around the 4th Century through China. and many people followed this ideology. Before the beginning of the JoSeon Dynasty, the 4th King, KwangJong (광종 光宗, 949-975) of the KoRyeo Dynasty (고려왕조 高麗王朝 : 918-1392) declared Buddhism as the state religion. However, in the end, Buddhist temples had too many land holdings, monk soldiers, and participated in a political power struggle, so the JoSeon Dynasty, which started during the 14th Century, rejected Buddhism and took Confucianism as the state religion. This placed monks in lower social and political positions in society and forced the temples to retreat to the deep mountain areas. Monks were even banned from entering the capitol city. Because of this manner of rule by the JoSeon Dynasty which continued for 500 years, Buddhism didn't have as much influence in Korean society as it did in

Japan. There were not many families holding funeral ceremonies in the Buddhist fashion, and there was no Danka system - (檀家制度 : support of Buddhist temple) - like there was in Japan.

However, Buddhism with a peaceful ideology had considerable influence on the people, and 23% of the nation today consider themselves as Buddhist or at least have some relationship to Buddhism. Although this thinking exists, only about half of them are doing things in the Buddhist way or holding Buddhist ceremonies for events in their lives. DongGuk University (동국대학교 東国大学校) is the most famous university with a relationship to Buddhism.

The Zhu Xi school of neo-Confucianism

Usually speaking, Confucianism was taught by Confucius, but originally that started by gathering Chinese philosophers' teachings which had continued from olden times, but as a matter of fact, Confucius just added his own thinking to those teachings to create what is now known as Confucianism. The core texts of Confucianism are the 4 Chinese Classics : Da Xue (大学), Lun Yu (論語), Meng Zi (孟子), and Zhong Yong (中庸). The contents taught people how to live their lives:

- Respect your parents
- Respect elders
- Hold good manners in high regard
- Be mindful of others
- Keep your word
- Avoid selfish desires and don't pursue only your own interests
- Do what you should do

This is the virtue of Confucianism.

It is often asked whether Confucianism is philosophy or religion, but Confucianism in the JoSeon Dynasty was the Zhu Xi school of neo-

Confucianism which has a really strong religious color. Confucianism started in the 6th Century BC, but more than 1600 years later in the 12th Century AD, Zhu Xi (朱熹, 1130-1200) annotated the 4 Chinese Classics and gave an even deeper meaning to the texts and created strict precepts. This is what is called the Zhu Xi school of neo-Confucianism. It can be said this person is the one who brought the beginning of the revival of Confucianism. The JoSeon Dynasty imported this Zhu Xi school of neo-Confucianism from the Song Dynasty (宋朝 : 960-1279) in China. Zhu Xi school of neo-Confucianism is called Song Xue (송학 宋学 : Song Philosophy), Xin Ru Xue (신유학 新儒学 : neo-Confucianism), and Xing Li Xue (성리학 性理学 : a theory of humanity and heavenly principles) in Japan and Korea. It also can be said that this is a kind of conservatism or the Right Wing within Confucianism.

Because the Zhu Xi school of neo-Confucianism had feudal ethics, it was a convenient system for the rulers. It contained non-democratic assertions which did not include the equality of people, human rights or other democratic ideals. For example the following:

- People had to be devoted to the king
- Children had to be dutiful to their parents
- The husband was the leader, the wife the follower
- Social status was defined from birth
- People should not try to cross the borders of their status
- Men and women are separated from age 7

The JoSeon Dynasty armed themselves theoretically with this Zhu Xi school of neo-Confucianism. The famous Ke Ju (科挙 : The test system of recruiting government workers) in China was started in the 6th Century. The Korean peninsula imported that system from KoRyeo Dynasty and the next dynasty, the JoSeon Dynasty, continued to use it as the national system and bureaucratized the governing system. In

China, the home of this bureaucracy, Confucianism was beginning to lose power step by step while the time is passing by and fell out of fashion at a remarkable rate by the time the Opium War (1839-42) began. In Japanese society, also Confucianism was seen as a combining of Buddhism and folk customs and it didn't grow as a single idea. Only the JoSeon Dynasty of the Korean peninsula raised it up as the state religion and exclusively developed the system of Confucianism and kept it in place by instituting a Closed Door Policy.

In the 18th Century at the time Catholicism arrived on the Korean peninsula, the JoSeon Dynasty persecuted them brutally. The reason was they felt there could not be or should not be any ideas better than Confucianism.

The Contents of Confucianism

For running the government, the JoSeon Dynasty educated and established many skilled bureaucrats (Nowadays these are high ranking officials.) These ranks were filled by those who studied Confucianism, so the JoSeon Dynasty continued with the system for a long time that was based on "the pen is mightier than the sword". Nowadays in Korea, this way of thinking is still a strong tradition. This means the JoSeon Dynasty already had a civilian control system in these earlier ages.

Men who were in the ruling group were studying diligently about Chinese written characters, Chinese poetry, and archery and trained in harshly restrictive courtesy and manners. They were also being educated in the Zhu Xi school of neo-Confucianism and had to pass a test on either the civil servant side or military side. This is the Ke Ju system. These made up the civil servant group and military group (a group was called 'ban (반 班)' in Korean.) These groups collectively

were generally called YangBan (양반 両班 : This means two groups, and the term was used to signify upper class or high social status.) Any person who passed this examination received a core position within the government system and was considered by the Korean people to have reached the greatest level of success in life. Passing that examination was too hard for entering YangBan society, and records show only 15,500 people passed it for a period that lasted the 519 years of the JoSeon Dynasty.

Someone who passed the Ke Ju examination and entered the YangBan society brought this honor and rise in status to their entire family. Someone who did not pass the examination still received the same kind of education and served for the king. Sons who belonged to the ruling ranks should:

- Not act in a lowly manner – avoiding avarice and miserly conduct
- Arise in the early morning
- Sit straightly and kneel while studying Chinese writings
- Never gamble

They were striving to keep these rules and to live a well-mannered daily life. The Christian church in modern Korean society has many early-morning prayer meetings or events of memorizing and presenting Bible scriptures. I think this comes from the historical environment.

In Korea there is still a famous university, SeongGyun-Gwan University (성균관대학교 成均館大学校), which is related to Confucianism which has a very long history. During the JoSeon Dynasty, in the capitol city there were four schools – East, West, South, and North – under the supervision of this university. Moreover, those graduates had a chance to take the Ke Ju examination. Furthermore, there was a school called HyangGyo (향교 鄉校 : local school) in every community, and they carried out the education system of the Zhu Xi school of neo-Confucianism for the sons of the YangBan there. Because of this, during the reign of the JoSeon Dynasty, many famous scholars appeared who were called DaeYu (대유 大儒 : Big Confucianist) and YuRim (유림 儒林 : group of Confucianist) who garnered much respect. JoSeon TongShinSa (조선통신사 朝鮮通信使) – those representatives who came to Japan in the Edo Period (1603-1867) as envoys for Korea were the people who got this kind of education. This is the background to why the JoSeon Dynasty was called the Gentlemen's Country of the East. Here the East means the far east of Eurasian land, and Gentleman means a person who is virtuous.

Confucianism nowadays still maintains a large influence in people's lives and customs but is of weaker influence than Buddhism. Consequently, since Confucianism isn't seen as religion, half of the Korean people do not think of themselves as being a religious person. However on the other hand, 35.7% of the people are Christian. It cannot be denied there is a strong impression of Korea as having a large population of Christians with this large of a percentage. Korea, a country who has a strong influence of Confucianism, suddenly greatly increased its Christian population to 35.7% from 7.7% in a period of about 30 years from 1960 to 1990. In reality, it can be said that half of the Koreans who come to Japan for business or tourism are Christian. What is the cause of this phenomenon? This is the theme of this book.

By the way, the Meiji government in Japan built up their position before their own country could be colonized and instituted a policy to colonize neighboring countries. For their fair defense of this policy, the Meiji government spread the image of Korean people of the JoSeon Dynasty as being of lower class and position than Japanese people, and even more they also gave the impression to their own people of Korea being a country of savages. I was born in the middle of World War II. At that time, many Japanese people held contemptuous ideas about Koreans and Chinese. My father was born in 1898 (Meiji 31st year). He was a prime example of someone who grew up under that kind of propaganda driven education system. If he were still living, he would now be 114 years old. This kind of derogatory and discriminatory education is not a story of long ago, but merely a short time ago historically.

In 1923 in the first of September, there was a large earthquake, Kanto Daishinsai (関東大震災). A groundless rumor against Koreans living there caused a vigilante organization to massacre the Korean people

14

living in that area. The number of killed was placed at 6,033. This was a result of the misguided education. However, in fact, the people of the JoSeon Dynasty had a very similar culture to Japanese culture and even a greater extent of being a higher, more well-mannered class than others.

Recently I consulted with a Japanese person who was preparing to marry a Korean. That consultation was about how to overcome the resistance to the marriage by the older Japanese relatives who still held on to their ingrained, slightly negative image of Koreans.

Section 2 – People's daily lives

Koreans of older times traditionally remained in the villages of their birth or lived in neighboring areas for their whole lives as was also the custom in Japan. Although the Tokugawa Period in Japan lasted 260 years in Japan, the JoSeon Dynasty lasted nearly twice as long at 519 years. Korea was an unchanging, closed society for a single family to stay close together with strong bonds. This ideal was held even more strongly than by the people of Japan.

Therefore, normal people for more than 500 years, family and relatives lived peacefully by helping each other even though they were very poor. Because of Korean people having rice as their main food, seasonal festivals followed the lunar calendar as in Japan. The Confucian ceremony JeSa (제사 祭祀 : memorials for ancestors performed several times a year) was held for events such as ChuSeok (추석 秋夕 : the fall harvest festival similar to Obon in Japan), YeonSi (연시 年始 : the first day of the year, similar to Gantan in Japan), KiJe (기제 忌祭 : memorials held on the day of a person's death), and sometimes were held in front of the ancestors' tombs or graves. In the eyes of the Japanese, these things were surprising due to the similarities between Korea and Japan.

The width of the area of present day South Korea is the same as the width of the Chubu area plus the Kinki area of Japan. It's about 25% of the width of all of Japan. Including North Korea, the width of area is about 60% of Japan. The Korean peninsula is divided by several mountain ranges, and there are many mountain ridges because there are so many mountains. Therefore there is a very clear separation of geological areas. This side of a mountain ridge is my home town, and the other side of the mountain ridge is like another country. This caused the natural growth of bonds between family members and relatives. This society had very strong relations between relatives.

70% of the Korean peninsula is made up of mountains, so only 30% of the land, which was the level country, held the greatest concentration of the population. The north side especially has more mountainous areas and the south side has a little more level ground in Seoul, BuSan and other areas. Geographically Korea is located slightly north of Japan. It has continental climate traits, so winter is dry and harshly cold.

Therefore they have developed a heating system, OnDol (온돌), to keep their homes warm which functions by heating the floors. There are no earthquakes like those in Japan.

You can see the buildings in BuSan from Japan.

It is easy to notice clearly when you see the map of the weather forecast on television every day how geographically close Korea is to Japan. The distance is only several hours by ship from Kyushu. When there is a typhoon, Japan and Korea are affected by strong winds at the same time. There are many places where you can see Mount Fuji from Tokyo, but the direct distance between Tokyo and Mount Fuji is about 100 kilometers. The distance between Tsusima (対馬) in Nagasaki Prefecture to BuSan City in South Korea is barely half that distance at about 50 kilometers. From that distance, on a clear day you can see the buildings in BuSan City.

Japanese are surprised by how similar their faces are to Koreans when visiting there. Although many people are unaware, average Korean height ranks in the upper, middle level of the world in comparison to other races. Generally their necks are thin and long, and back muscles are well-developed. Therefore there are many people with fairly straight posture and are well-proportioned in body shape, so sometimes you can tell if someone is not Japanese by someone's gate as they walk. Of course there are also those who do not fit that body shape. When I am on the train, I do not feel Koreans and Japanese are from different countries or that I am a foreigner or outsider. Scenery in the countryside is also very similar. Trees, plants, and flowers growing there are also very similar. It is a foreign country, but it feels very close and similar to you. However, Korean character is completely different from Japanese character. You could even say that it is completely opposite in nature.

Character of Ethnic Koreans is completely different from that of Japanese

Ethnic character is shaped by climate. Except for during the summer season, the mornings in Korea have little humidity and a soft cool breeze. The word "JoSeon" expresses this condition of the climate very well. The difference of the four seasons is set off more clearly than in Japan. In the spring there is an overabundance of blooming azaleas. In the fall, the people enjoy watching the changing of the colors of the leaves. There is little humidity which is due to the Korean peninsula having a continental climate. Compared to Japan, the sky is clear and beautiful. In the winter there is a coldness that is felt as deep as the bone. This climate makes the character of ethnic Koreans to not be antagonistic. When they have an opinion to share they speak out. They say "yes" clearly about good things, and they say "no" just as clearly when they disagree with something. The Korean culture base is similar to the Japanese cultural base, but they differ in this area of mentality.

Japanese character traits include diligence, sincerity, calmness, a preference for pastel colors, modesty, and they do not display emotion.

On the other hand, Korean character traits include passion, devotion, activeness, a preference for bold, basic colors, self-assertiveness, and they display their emotions.

Japanese living in a small island country had no other choice than to live with much consideration of other people and working to keep peace between them. However, the people on the Korean peninsula are living on a continent. They do not hesitate to speak out loudly about their own opinions. Self-assertiveness is one of the common ingredients of their character. They cry in front of others, get angry, and express their displeasure openly. From a Japanese point of view like mine, it seems their ethnic character has a pureness and honesty like a small child.

The character of Korean people in a social context is similar to Westerners. While Japanese are not saying yes or no clearly, Koreans do say. I think in international society it is far easier for Koreans to be accepted than for Japanese. Japanese have two different sides with one being internal intentions and the other being the external intentions, but Koreans are not this way. What they say is what they mean. While Japanese are saying their opinion thoughtfully, Koreans are saying directly. This directness may also be more welcomed in international society. In that same way, Koreans are not so sensitive but have the continental climate character traits of generosity and liberality. This type of character comes from the climate and geography of the Korean peninsula.

All relatives constitute a family in Korea

According to research done in 1995, in Korea there are only 272 different family names (Japan has about 130,000) and 35 varieties of the family names of Kim (김 金), Lee (이 李), Park (박 朴), Choe (최 崔), and Jeong (정 鄭) which take up 90% of the 272 total. Confucianism places regard for parents as the most important tenet, so whole and extended families lived in the same village. This kind of custom lasted for more than 500 years, so a person who lived in the same village might face the risk of extended family members marrying. To help to avoid this problem, people in Korea of the same family name and same ancestry were not allowed to marry.

July 16th of 1997 the Constitutional Court of Korea ruled that the law prohibiting the marriage of people who had the same family name and ancestry as stated in Civil Law, Article 809, Item 1 was unconstitutional. Arguments about this are still continuing in Korea, but in Civil Law, Article 815, it was established that relatives from less than the 8th degree were prohibited from marriage. On the other hand, those who had the same family name and ancestry are called relatives without exception, and this bond is so strong that foreigners have difficulty understanding it. Even at present, there is an island which has many people marrying others within the island, and the people there have a saying "SaDon, there is nobody you can call outsiders among 'SaDon'." "SaDon" is the term for addressing each other between the parents-in-law of a married couple. This means that all of the people who live on that island are relatives or family.

Most Korean people have their own JokBo (족보 族譜). JokBo means the chart which shows the family lineage. It can be seen very clearly the difference between those who are blood relatives and others who are not blood relatives. Some people say you can trace even more than 30 generations on this JokBo. I think this is because of people not often moving to other areas due to the mountainous terrain and relatives continued to live in the same place. Thus, you can easily trace family lineage in the JoSeon Dynasty. Society established that blood relationships were so strong which is at a level nearly beyond belief to Japanese. Then, in the middle of the 18th century, the family tree which you can see in use today was completed.

A group of people in Korea with the same family name and ancestry was called "MoonJung (문중 門中)". In present day Korea, there are many people who are living outside of their home towns and commuting for work and other reasons to other communities, and they call the regular gatherings of these people "MoonJung-Hwe (문중회 門中会)" that is called "relatives meeting" in Japan. They gather often for social functions such as job fairs, house moving, and funeral ceremonies and help each other.

In Korea it was common for religious memorial ceremonies to be held for up to four generations of people who had passed away – great-great grandparents, great grandparents, grandparents, and parents. These memorial ceremonies "KiJe" were held on the night of the day before the anniversary of their passing. In the Confucianism way, that ceremony starts at 12:00 midnight. First the main gate and windows are opened (This is for inviting the spirit), put away laundry poles (so as not to trip the spirit), preparing food offerings, burning incense, and lighting candles. Also several times they offered servings of alcohol and deeply bowing dozens of times placing their forehead to the floor, and reading or reciting ritual prayers of respect to the ancestors. The ceremony usually lasts for about 30 minutes according to the Confucianism way.

Worshipping their ancestors in the manner of Confucianism is a part of the core Korean identity. I will talk more about this later, but a long time ago the Japanese government forced them to adopt Japanese style names for their name and family names which is so rude of them when you consider how important Koreans hold this tradition of maintaining their family names and how treasured they held the ideal of keeping their family and relationships.

In 1947 in Japan according to the new constitution, the Koshu (戸主) system was abolished. (this system placed a headmaster in each family), but in Korea this system continued until 2008 and replaced it with the "HoJeok (호적 戸籍)" system which established an individual family registry. To establish this new system took a very long time, and there were many Confucianism groups who opposed it. A trend of treasuring individual rights began to appear in not only in the Korean people's thoughts but in the governing system as well. In other words, Korea slowly changed from a Korea with a male-dominated society like that of Japan and the change is still taking place. In 2005, the percentage of women attending college was over 80% and the number of those who worked after marriage also increased.

Depth of Human Feelings – warm-heartedness

If you go to Korea, you can see male high school students walking hand in hand with their mothers. In Japan male high school students would feel uncomfortable in this situation. In Korea interpersonal relationships are far different from Japanese interpersonal relationships. If a Japanese woman marries a Korean man, she will be surprised by the fact their mother-in-law may enter their home without prior notice or contact. They treat daughters-in-law the same as their real daughters. Koreans say "there's no courtesy needed between those who are close" and it is the opposite of the Japanese custom for this. Koreans' interpersonal relationships are very close even to those outside their family, and they feel a warm-heartedness to all of the people who are near them. Japanese also have this kind of custom about their feelings, but Koreans feel this more deeply than Japanese.

To Japanese there are the special expressions "Wabi" or "Sabi". "Wabi" means having an austere refinement while "Sabi" means having quiet, simplistic grace. These words mean enjoying a quiet life or express a quiet atmosphere, yet Korea does not have these kinds of expressions. They express directly what is seen or felt. They prefer bold, basic colors such as red, yellow, and blue.

With this kind of ethnic character and a long history of being ruled by Confucianism, Koreans' person to person relationships are developed through many complicated elements. Because it was a dynastic system, people who had government posts were held in high regard and respected by people, and they placed great importance on titles. This image is very easy to grasp since Japan is very similar in this manner. Nowadays in Korea there is still a very strict pecking order in society based on social factors such as age, status, or relationships. Following this pecking order is vital in every situation and direction, and honorific language is highly developed. Therefore, keeping one's honor by following these mores is a very important custom, and the key is it requires a person to act appropriately by seeing the mind of others' very well. This was learned through exposure to these acts which was not affected by being Christian.

When first meeting, confirmation is made of family name, given name, age, and whether there is any blood relationship. Next confirmation is made about other personal history such as hometown or which school was graduated. Based on these responses, the relationship between oneself and another is shown by the word choice and actions towards each other. When someone enters a company as a new employee, the relationship between workers is greatly affected by whether there is a previous relationship or not and the depth of it. Cliques or social circles are created based on this kind of background. In Korea, this often occurs though in Japan it is not as prevalent. Moreover, the relationship between superiors and subordinates is very clearly set, so it is essential for each person to maintain both the honor of the individual and that of the group. In other words, Koreans think it is very important to maintain the honor of those they are related to by blood, those with whom they have a shared territorial bond, or school alumni. These days this way of thinking is strongly adhered to, but it was much stronger during the JoSeon Dynasty.

Commoners – regular citizens

In the JoSeon Dynasty, the commoners' lives were governed by the teachings and customs of Confucianism.

The head of the family was the father, and that position was passed on to the eldest son:

- Commoners had to follow the ruler
- They had to show respect to their elders
- They should not try to cross the border of their status
- They should keep good manners
- They should arise in the early morning and work

These tenets were held in high regard. Even though the lifestyles were very different between the Upper Class and Commoners, their basic thinking was ruled by the same ideas (Confucianism). The climate had little humidity, their character was influenced by "continental character", and there were four distinct seasons which were more clearly separated than in Japan; these factors along with Confucianism made up the character of ethnic Koreans.

The JoSeon Dynasty was based on moral teachings about self-control but also included some inconsistencies. One of which was the sadness from being so poor.

When it comes to the idea of being poor, someone raised in Japan also has many familiar experiences of being poor. When I was an elementary school student, just after World War II ended, in the classroom there were some students who could not afford to bring their own lunches. Those who could not afford lunches spent their time around the pull-up bar in the corner of the playground during lunch time. Oh, what kind of feelings would those children have had at that time? There was also the poorness at Ganpeki of Maizuru Port where I once lived. I still don't know what became of "the mother from Ganpeki (岸壁の母)" who was waiting for her son who had not returned yet from the battlefield. There is also an Uncle who as his business carried a large bamboo basket on his back and travelled all around Japan by train. How few were the times within a year where he was able to return to his own home?

Maybe it was only once or twice. I grew up during a time when Japan was so poor. There were many detestable incidents, sad incidents.

In the JoSeon Dynasty, those commoners who lived in Seoul, the capitol, were also very poor. Even more than these, the commoners who lived in the countryside had few chances for education. They mainly lived all of their lives by doing agricultural work, raising livestock, fishing, making handicrafts, and conducting small commercial trade. At times, a famine, a drought, or a large storm such as a typhoon came upon them. The difficulty of a commoner's life was not that different from those of the olden ages of Japan. Still you can feel there was too much of a gap between the difficulties of living a life so poor that death was seen as a relief and the high-mindedness of the, sublime teachings of Confucianism.

The Song "Arirang"

There is a very famous folk song called "Arirang". There are several different opinions about the meaning of the word "Arirang". One highly regarded opinion is that it is the name of a mountain pass.

Arirang, Arirang, Arariyo. 아리랑, 아리랑, 아라리요.

Arirang gogero neomeoh ganda ----- 아리랑 고개로 넘어간다.

This is translated in English as:

Arirang, Arirang, Arariyo,

Go over the Pass on Arirang Mountain

The first lines of the song are repeated and then a variety of many different verses follow. All of these are a style of song called Arirang. These verses are about different themes such as unrequited love, dissatisfaction with the state of the world, ill will, or love for a hometown, and there are more than 2000 verses. It is not known which verses are the actual verses of the original song. The songs' melodies are also similar yet have more than 100 variations, and it is also not known which of these melodies the original is. I also have heard more than 10 different melodies up until now.

It can't be said when or where this song was first sung. It is said however that in the 1860's, DaeWon-Goon (대원군 大院君 : When there was no direct successor to the throne, someone was chosen from the king's family. DaeWon-Goon was the title given to the father of the one selected.), HeungSeon (흥선 興宣) rebuilt the main palace, KyeongBok-Goong (경복궁 慶福宮). He drafted workers from all over the country, and those people started to sing this song. Daewon-Goon was cheered by hearing this song being sung, and it became widespread. It was a beautiful melody with a sad feeling, and Daewon-Goon loved that song and allowed them to sing it.

There was a silent movie titled "Arirang" that was an original film and was directed by Nah OonGyu (나운규 羅雲圭 : 1902-1937). The original film described the sadness of separation by poverty and the resistance to Japanese Imperialism and persecution during the time Korea was being colonized by Japan. At the time of its showing, the film was wildly popular and received with great enthusiasm.

The story of this movie is about the main character, YeongJin (영진), losing his mind due to the harshness of his daily life and killing those who persecuted his family. (These persecutors were hinted to be Japanese.) At the last, the murderer was arrested by the police and the picture then faded away. The lyrics of the theme song Arirang of the same titled movie was written by the director himself and became an explosive hit. In 1931 in Japan this movie was translated into Japanese as "Arirang Song" and distributed by the Victor entertainment company and became famous.

The first time I heard this song was after World War II when I was an elementary school student. It was so sad and so beautiful that once you heard that song, it lingered around your ear. For example in comparison, it carries the same impression as the song in Japan called Itsuki-no Komori Uta (五木の子守歌 : Itsuki's Lullaby), but it sounds more melancholy than even that. What kind of sadness lay behind this song? Even though they had the sublime mental teachings of Confucianism, under these harsh conditions of poverty and persecution the minds of those commoners were earnestly expressed by this song.

When you see Japan, China, and Korean history, all of those countries have many harsh and sad instances brought about by the same feudalistic ideals. Natural disasters such as famines or floods caused the deaths of many poor people, small babies were killed in order to help other siblings to survive, girls were sold, and the elderly were cast out into the mountains. Arirang is a commoners' song written at the time when only royal families enjoyed the extremes of luxury and commoners suffered the extremes of poverty. The song included expressions of the commoners' daily lives, loves, and many separations. From the end of the JoSeon Dynasty to the Japanese Imperial reign, time changed but the mountain pass of the commoners' sadness continued as seen in the lyrics of the Arirang Song. Under these kinds of conditioners, Christianity entered the Korean peninsula.

Section 3 – Christian Missionaries and the History of Martyrdom

Here I will simplistically explain about the basic elements of Christian beliefs. Christianity is a religion that believes Jesus Christ is God's son. God's son, what can you say God's son is? Furthermore, what kind of relationship does God's son have with God?

What are Christian Beliefs?

To explain it in simple terms, the relationship between God and Christ is comparable to freshly made "Mochi" (gluttonized rice cake). If it is freshly made Mochi, you can tear it off by hand and eat. The torn off piece of Mochi can be compared to Christ, and the remaining piece can be compared to God the Father. If it is still warm, the small piece can be reattached to the original piece to form one, smooth piece again. The character of both pieces is the same. In this way, God the Father and Jesus Christ are the same God. When Jesus Christ came to this world, God the Father and Christ were separate beings. However, after Christ finished his work in this world, he returned to the side of God.

Christianity is the belief in two gods at once, but you cannot say they are two different gods as they are essentially one God. This is because Christ was originally in God the Father. You could say that when God the Father created the universe, the Christ in God the Father also created the universe together with him. In this meaning, Christianity believes Christ is the son of God the Father.

When the Son of God was sent to this earthly world, he was delivered like an animal in a manger, a poor animal's house, the poorest of places, and when he died, he had to die on the cross, one of the most cruel and pitiful forms of death. This is in order to show God's deep love and humbleness towards mankind. When Korean people heard this story of Christ, they were greatly moved.

He always had the nature of God... He became like a human being and appeared in human likeness. He was humble and walked the path of obedience all the way to death – his death on the cross. (Philippians 2: 6-8)

To explain further, Christians pray to one God, God the Father and Jesus Christ together. The Holy Spirit that is not seen is sent from this oneness of God to believers, and believers are praying under the aid of this Holy Spirit. If you have this kind of God image in your mind, when you are anywhere, anytime, believers can pray even in an airplane, on the top of a mountain, or in the kitchen.

The biggest number of martyrs in the world

On the Korean peninsula there were no Christian missionaries from Portugal or Spain in the 16th Century as there were in Japan. They were so completely isolated from the outside world that a missionary could not enter even a single step. Christianity entered the Korean peninsula more than 250 years after Japan, and it was started by missionaries of the modern age Catholic Church.

An officer, Yi SeungHoon (이승훈 李承薰), an envoy to China of the JoSeon Dynasty became a believer in God, and in 1784 he returned to Korea. Later the Catholic Church in Korea established this year was the starting year for missionaries. Within 5 years of his and other new believers' beginning to spread the word, the number of Christians in

Korea grew to about 4,000 people. An important point about the Korean Catholic Church was for the first 50 years of existing in Korea there was not even one Catholic Priest due to the government policy of isolationism. In other words, only believers carried out this mission of Christianity to others. This is an astonishing fact. This is similar to the clandestine movement of Christianity in Japan during the Tokugawa Period which maintained their belief for more than 270 years.

However, the JoSeon government persecuted the new Catholic believers and attacked the places where they worshipped and dispersed the gatherings. The year after the beginning of the missionary movement in Korea, the first person was martyred, and his name was Kim BeomTo (김범토 金範兎). Today, the main Catholic Church in Korea, MyeongDong Cathedral (명동성당 明洞聖堂), is built upon the land where his house stood.

This was the start, and from the 19th Century in Korea there was a great and cruel persecution of Catholic believers which lasted for 70 years.

First Great Persecution (1801)

Including the officer who was the first believer in Korea, 300 people were executed. In spite of this great persecution, in 1837 the number of believers increased to about 9,000 people.

Second Great Persecution (1839-40)

113 people were executed

Third Great Persecution (1866)

According to records in the book HanGuk TongSa (한국통사 韓国痛 史 : Korean Grievous History) there were 120,000 people executed, but a more believable number is probably about 8,000. However, including those who died from hunger and cold the number could be tens of thousands.(1)

Fourth Great Persecution (1871)

The number of people executed is not clear.

The year 1871 when these great persecutions ended was the fourth year of the Meiji Era in Japan. This great persecution of Catholic believers in Korea occurred in Modern Ages, not in the Middle Ages as in Japan. Most Koreans learned of this in school and know of the history of persecution in Korea, and many live near a place where these persecutions happened. This is a very familiar topic for them.

Winter is too cold restricting travel, and being geographically located on the far east side of the continent caused the JoSeon government to resist the entrance of Christianity and made it easier for them to block it. However the number of those who were executed certainly numbered in the tens to hundreds of thousands even by a low count. Surely it is such that it is an unbelievably high number. That persecution in the Korean peninsula would be more than the notorious persecution during the Roman rule. C. H. Robinson, a church historian, wrote about the ordeals of the Korean Catholic Church, "you simply cannot say whether or not Christians during the old ages of the Roman rule suffered more than Korean Christians suffered from the first of the 19th Century for 70 years".(2)

A grain of wheat

In that small peninsula, in that age where the population at that time was not as much as it is today, the fact that much martyrdom took place is a point of pride for Koreans today. Korean nationally known novelist Yi GwangSoo (이광수 李光洙), similar to someone like Natsume Souseki (夏目漱石) in Japan, in 1935 said:

I respect the martyred Catholics who numbered in the tens of thousands. It is very shameful though we know so little about that. The fact that Koreans had so many people who were martyrs is a point of pride that will last forever, and when I think about the blood of those martyred flows in my veins, I feel strong and very proud. (3)

The persecution of Christians resulted in producing more Christians which was opposite to the idea of the rulers. One of the Japanese images of Christianity likely is also an image of respect because Christians were willing to give up their lives in the 16th century in order to save their religion. In Nagasaki 26 people were martyred which included an eleven year old boy. Someone told a story about a samurai who took them from Osaka to Nagasaki thought it was too cruel to kill that innocent boy and several times admonished the boy to say "I am not a believer". However, after they arrived to Nagasaki, at the place of execution the boy said, "Uncle, my cross is that small one?" and went towards that cross.

Martyrdom rather than being an expectation of a heroic death or just giving up on this world required the inner strength to pass beyond the panic of death. In the Bible, if someone has that strong of a belief, God would send a Holy Spirit and the person would be made even stronger in their convictions. Christians would say that it was a "gift of the Holy Spirit" (I Corinthians 12:9).

The church father Tertullianus (c.160–c.225) who defended Christians against the Roman rulers in his book "Apologeticus" says:

The more you persecute us, our believers would be doubled. And "the blood of the martyrs is the seed of the Church".(4)

The key point of Tertullian's words is that the blood of martyrs is never wasted. It would be the same as a single seed begetting much fruit because a single martyr had great influence on many people's beliefs and thoughts about Christians and helped to convert them to Christianity. This would be proved by the great increase of numbers of Korean Catholic believers which I will write more about ater. In the words of Jesus Christ there is proof of this as Christ himself foretold his own life being sacrificed upon the cross:

Most assuredly, I say to you, unless a grain of wheat falls into the ground and dies, it remains alone; but if it dies, it produces much grain. (John 12:24)

Section 4 PyeongYang (평양 平壤) was called "the Jerusalem of the East"

The JoSeon Dynasty lasted for 500 years, and after all the opening of the country occurred due to the demand by Japan, America and European countries for them to open their doors. It happened in 1876 (the 9th Year of the Meiji Era). After that historical change happened rapidly.

- 1894-1895 The Sino-Japanese War (The war for gaining supremacy over the Korean Peninsula fought on the Korean peninsula, Manchuria, and the Liao Dong peninsula in China. Japan won.)
- 1904-1905 The Russo-Japanese War (The war of gaining supremacy over the Korean Peninsula between Russia and Japan mainly fought on Manchuria, the Korean peninsula and on the Yellow Sea. Japan won.)
- 1907 Disarmament of the JoSeon Dynasty Army by the Japanese government
- 1910 JoSeon Dynasty collapsed (Colonized by Japan.)

From the opening of the country to the fall to colonization there was only 34 short years. This disarmament especially carried a feeling of great insult to all the leaders of Korea including the YangBan. Those people of the JoSeon Dynasty who had enjoyed the extremes of luxury for 519 years were left in a state of shock. There had been no civil war, they hadn't started a war, and yet suddenly the Japanese, though foreigners, entered the Korean peninsula and made their land a battlefield for fighting with China and Russia, so this was traumatic.

Some of the people didn't accept the disarmament and resisted by raising a loyal army with their personal weapons and going underground. Normal citizens didn't know what they could do and had no other choice than to submit to the Japanese army. This kind of great change was like sudden thunder appearing from clear skies to an innocent boy who followed the Zhu Xi school of neo-Confucianism. At that time the entire population of Korea was only about 13,000,000. For comparison, the total population of Japan was about 49,000,000.

Missionaries enter Korea

At the time the Japanese army entered Korea, something else entered Korea. It was protestant Christianity. Catholic Christianity which already existed in Korea was under persecution, but the history was also already 100 years old. In Korea, Catholic Christianity was called "CheonJu-Gyo "(천주교 天主教 : The Teachings of the Heavenly Lord), and Protestant Christianity was called "GaeShin-Gyo" (개신교 改新教 : New Teachings of the Heavenly Lord). These two movements were thought of as two separate and different teachings.

In the JoSeon Dynasty, the first Protestant missionary to enter the Korean peninsula was an American doctor, Horace Allen, and it was 1884 (the 17th year of the Meiji Era). It was exactly one hundred years after Catholic missionaries began there in 1784. Furthermore, in the next year, 1885 an American, Southern Presbyterian Pastor, Horace Underwood (July 19, 1859 - October 12, 1916), Methodist Pastor Henry Appenzeller (February 6, 1858 – June 11, 1902), and Methodist missionary Doctor William Scranton (1856-1922) were on the same ship bound for Korea. This moment marks the beginning of Protestant missions.

The Presbyterian sect has restrictive doctrine which came from the Reformer John Calvin, and it has the largest number of believers in the world belonging to the church of this sect. More than half of the Korean Protestant churches belong to this sect.

The Methodist sect holds the scripture as reverently as the Presbyterians but emphasizes the work of the Holy Spirit (invisible, but God's power). The structure of the Methodist church places a president to watch over the group as the prime leader after the manner of the Catholic church. In Korea they are calling this GamNi GyoHwe (감리교회 監理教会). These two biggest sects make up the majority of Protestant churches.

If someone is not a Christian, it would not be easy to understand the differences between these sects, yet it is not necessary to separate these sects specifically. As a matter of fact, I'm a pastor and have worked in both of these sects, the Presbyterian and Methodist. The difference of these sects to put it simply is much like comparing the differences of two schools. One school is following traditional rules and the rules are very strict, while the other has a free and bright atmosphere. The Protestant church has more than 100 sects, but the primary beliefs and teachings have no differences. Over several centuries in many different countries there have been many different missionaries, so it is a very natural thing there are many different names for the sects.

The influence of Puritans and Spiritual Belief

The first missionaries to enter Korea were Pastor Underwood, who was 26 years old at the time, and he had studied at New York University which was influenced greatly by Puritan beliefs, and also Pastor Appenzeller who graduated from Drew Theological Seminary which emphasized experiencing the Holy Spirit which is reflected in Methodist beliefs. The two missionaries were well-educated under the influence of both the Puritan and Spiritual beliefs. This is deeply reflected in the

Korean Protestant church. Their belief was very pure and innocent.

Puritanism is not a sect of Christianity. In 1534, 17 years after the Reformation lead by Luther, in England there was also a similar movement. The King of England, Henry VIII, lead this Reformation and established independence by separating from the Catholic Church and creating the Church of England which chose their own path. However, it was an imperfect reformation, so there were some believers from the beginning that did not accept the change. Especially in a moral way there were some believers who wanted to strictly adhere to the rules. They were called Puritans in English and were related to the "Kathari" sect (katheros in Greek means 'pure') which started in the middle ages.

In other words, Puritan was a label placed on the group which emphasized moral pureness and the teachings of restrictive doctrine. A part of this group of people immigrated to the new world in America to realize their religious dream and contributed to the settling of the United States of America. Then their descendants were the ones who were in the first missionaries to enter the Korean peninsula, Underwood and Appenzeller. Up until present day, this kind of puritanical belief of the first missionaries continues to have a great affect on the Korean protestant church. It is characterized by:

- Belief in the words of the Bible reverently and not interpreting them in a different way
- Living purely – no alcohol, no smoking
- Strictly keep Sundays for worship
- Emphasize the mighty work of the Holy Spirit

Missionaries taught about God's love, strict puritanical morals, and a strict way of life to those commoners who had strict Confucian morals and led lives of poverty. In other words, strict and sincere missionaries brought in Christianity to strict and sincere people. Said differently, very pure and innocent missionaries taught the pure and innocent word and teachings of the Bible to a very pure and innocent race. In this sense of pureness the two went well together. It must be the missionaries success came from this compatibility of their way of life and these teachings.

The Commoners' writing character 'Hangul' and Christian missionaries

In Japan, if you enter elementary school, students are first taught to write using the "Kana" characters "I-Ro-Ha". Hiragana is the simple form of Japanese writing, and with the 48 written characters of I-Ro-Ha you can write any sentence. Korean written characters of Hangul are less than this, and with only 40 characters you can write any sentence you can pronounce. Therefore it is much less complicated than Japanese Hiragana.

These simplistic written characters of Hangul are in fact fairly new and were created during the reign of the 4th King, SeJong, of the JoSeon Dynasty in 1446 for educating commoners. This is only about 560 years ago. However, the people of the JoSeon Dynasty didn't see this use as being important. They were using difficult and complex written characters of Hanja (based on Chinese characters) and looked down on the simplicity of Hangul. You can say there was an arrogance of the upper class.

Japanese and Korean language is similar in usage. For example in Japanese if you say, "Sodesune" (そうですね : "That's right, huh?"), the reply is not only sometimes "Yes" but sometimes "No". In Korean you would say, "Geureoseyo" (그러세요), and you can also answer in the same way. Both languages are peculiarly ambiguous. Chinese written characters also have this kind of nature. In the Chinese writing system one character can have more than 30 different meanings. In Japan and on the Korean peninsula both, they successfully changed the

Chinese written characters to their own way of reading and pronouncing them and mixed them along with their own native languages to fit their usage. Japanese and Korean languages also both based 70% of their total vocabularies on these Chinese characters.

The Protestant church began to put Hangul to use extensively. The Protestant church holds the scriptures of the Bible as the most important aspect. You can say this is a religion of scripture. In church they had used Hangul in the translated Bible, for making documents, and for spreading the gospel to propagate their mission. A Korean scholar, Ham SeokHeon, (함석헌 咸錫憲 : 1901-1989) in his book "On This Road Till I Die" (죽을 때까지 이 걸음으로) said about his mother:

(My mother) came to believe in Jesus after she turned 50 years old. She learned Hangul and became a good reader of the Bible, but when she was young she was a woman who didn't know any written characters.(5)

Up until just several years ago, you could easily meet this kind of person who had learned Hangul in the church and who was pleased by being able to read. However, it was not only church people who had begun to use Hangul. Newspapers began publishing in Hangul, and public education materials were also using the Hangul writing system. In society at that time, the leaders and influential people included many Christians. Nowadays, the protestant church has this background which has resulted in the group being so big. This was partly caused by the church teaching Christianity to the people by using Hangul. In Japanese thinking, using Kana, I-Ro-Ha and Chinese characters together is the normal way, so using Hangul and Chinese characters together must be very practical. However in Korean language, by using only Hangul, it is possible to express your thoughts, so you can omit the difficulty of learning Chinese characters. To Koreans this is a very important point of convenience. Hangul was not created in the olden ages, but was created in the 15th century. In 1997, Hangul was designated as a national treasure by UNESCO as a "Memory of the World".

Missionaries on the Korean Peninsula used the "Nevius Style"

1890 was about five years after the first time Protestant missionaries arrived on the Korean peninsula. The number of American missionaries was growing, and they opened a conference for studying about missionaries by inviting as a lecturer a missionary who had been working in China for a long time. That lecturer was American missionary John Nevius (1829-1893) who was very experienced and already more than 60 years old. He was sent to China by the Presbyterian Church. He first went to China when he was 25 and stayed there until his death there at age 64. He devoted his entire adult life to being a missionary to the Chinese.

Koreans since the time they first believed in Jesus Christ have thought it was important for believers to share with others their belief in Christ and invite them to attend church. Nevius had a deep insight into the innocence and pureness of the Korean character.

His opinion was for the Korean people who didn't agree with the idea of doing something for others for money, in other words they were the "Gentlemen's Country of the East", that missionaries should just teach the Bible and then allow the Korean people to act independently and manage themselves and be responsible for their own means and supplies for maintaining their new churches.

In the JoSeon Dynasty there was the thought called "SeonBi JeongShin" (선비정신)similar to that of Bushido (武士道) in Japan. "SeonBi" means the one with deep knowledge and the power to act, and so is a superior person among the human race. Nevius taught those missionaries the method listed above to people who have this kind of thinking it is better to use an approach to the mind.

Furthermore, he said they should appoint Korean pastors as quickly as possible and support that pastor by the offering of believers. In other words, Nevius taught the missionaries who went to Korea for spreading the word of Christianity never to support their cause by money they supplied themselves. This theory for Korean missionaries was very suitable when you think of the character of the Korean people.

In 1908, just 24 years after the coming of missionaries, there is data that shows the number of Protestant Churches during the JoSeon Dynasty just before its collapse. There were 188 churches, and 186 of them were self-sufficient.(6) Believers supported the churches with generous offerings even though they were very poor. This kind of mind continues still in the Korean church.

In the Bible, Jesus Christ taught that people should go to other places and spread the word of the Gospel (Matthew 28:19). The people of the Korean peninsula also soon sent missionaries abroad. September 17th, 1907 is an important day which is remembered as the anniversary of 7 young Korean people who were ordained as pastors of the Presbyterian Church. One of them though not sent abroad was sent to JeJu Island which had no missionaries before this time. I have a photograph that was taken at that moment to commemorate the event. The picture is of several people all wearing white clothes and hats. Even though these first seven pastors were very important workers for their respective churches, because they believed the Bible's word about it being necessary to send missionaries in order to be a complete church, they couldn't bend from this requirement and sent one pastor as a missionary. At the present time, Korean churches send the second most missionaries abroad. This is not a trend just of today, but it has been like this from the beginning. I think it certainly is an illustrative story about Koreans' ethnic character. Recently there are also many Korean pastors who have been sent as missionaries to Japan and other countries all over the world.

The next thing Nevius recommended was about studying the Bible systematically for all believers of the church. This included not only private Bible study, but also that everyone should gather together in order to study. This kind of Bible study meeting was called "SaGyeong-Hwe" (사경회 査経会 : this means "Checking the Bible Meeting"), and believers were educated strictly in accordance with the words of the Bible.

Furthermore, Nevius insisted that for all church activities the word of the Bible should be followed down to the smallest of details. In Japanese churches every kind of leader is called "Yakuin" (director), but in Korean churches they are not using such ambiguous titles and there are different titles based on the Bible's teachings such as "JangNo" (장로 長老 : "Elder") or "JipSa" (집사 執事 : "Deacon"). That is to say those Orthodox principles cover every single church activity even to the smallest. Korean character is to express one's self directly and practice with passion, so the ideals Nevius put forth are very suitable.

Another thing Nevius advised about was the idea of support by the group for missionaries of other churches. He recommended they work together rather than being in competition for who could establish their church first. Because having two churches in a small town or village was not economical, one should move to another place in order to spread Christianity with a spirit of cooperation and all missionaries should work together. This was very practical advice.

I have the experience of being a missionary to a small town in the countryside of Japan. In this small town there were already 4 established churches. All 4 of those were very small churches and should have been united as one, but each one had already developed their tradition and history for decades which made it difficult for them to merge as one.

However, 5 years after the first missionaries started, during the first period of the Korean Protestant church, this became a reality as missionaries began working together in cooperation with other missionaries following this conference. The recommendations of Nevius were rich with foresight.

The contents of this conference which had invited Nevius as a lecturer later became known as "Nevius Style": self-sufficient church activities, sending missionaries abroad, churches governed strictly by the words of the Bible, a spirit of cooperation between different denominations, and the spreading of the word of Christianity to commoners. These are held up in the Korean Protestant Church as a good tradition. When it comes to the present churches of Korea, which are made up of many denominations and are many in number, in regards to the spirit of cooperation, it is not easy to say this mutual consent still exists in practice, but the other aspects are still important facets in action.

PyeongYang —was called "the Jerusalem of the East"

PyeongYang, which is located 200 kilometers to the north of the Korean capitol Seoul, at the time was the main base of missionaries of the American Northern Presbyterian Church (the American Presbyterian church was separated into Northern and Southern divisions). The famous PyeongYang Seminary (the only seminary of the time for educating pastors for the Presbyterian Church) was built there. The first group of important pastors was produced by this seminary. By comparison, PyeongYang would be like the cities of Senda or Morioka in Japan. It was a beautiful city full of green. Along with Seoul, this is also a very important city to the people who live on the Korean peninsula.

About 10 years after that conference was held with Nevius, those missionaries and the first group of Korean leaders harvested the fruit of the actions from the Nevius style applied in PyeongYang. Those Christians who for 10 years had studied the words of the Bible, in around 1903, in WonSan (원산 元山), a city located on the northern side of the East Sea coast, experienced the movement of the Holy Spirit between the missionaries and believers and enjoyed a special atmosphere with their passionate belief. The experience of the Holy Spirit was seen through the healing of sickness, speaking in tongues, suddenly having the ability to speak a language different from their native language, and being covered in a special pleasant feeling. The next experience was in 1907 by the pastors and believers in PyeongYang.

1907 was the year of the disarmament of the JoSeon Dynasty army by the Japanese government and the continuation of colonization efforts step by step. In America in 1712 the descendants of the Puritans experienced the Holy Spirit in the same way. After that this kind of experience sometimes occurred, so the missionaries from America understood about the experience of this miracle and could accurately guide the Korean Christians.

Usually if someone has this kind of experience, they were insulted or hated by other people because this kind of experience isn't theoretical, and it sometimes incited fighting within the church and caused division within the church followers. However as I've mentioned before the church on the Korean peninsula was filled with Puritanical belief, so the church in PyeongYang was moved by the Holy Spirit over a long period of time. That city was filled with people who worshiped and prayed, and it took on the manner of a Holy City. PyeongYang was called "the Jerusalem of the East" founded on this history. In the Christian church, this kind of situation is called "revival" (live again – in Korean this is called "BuHeong" (부흥 復興), and revival came from the words of the Bible in the 2nd Chapter of Acts where the Holy Spirit came down.

This situation lasted for several years, and in the end it had influence on many other areas. In 1890 there were only 169 believers in the Protestant church in Korea, and within just 20 years by around 1910 the number had rapidly increased to about 160,000 believers (believers of the Catholic Church were just under 40,000). At present in Korea, the reason the Protestant church is very strong is because from the beginning of the work of the missionaries all of these elements fit together very well. The population of PyeongYang of that time was thought to be from 40,000 to 50,000, and the number of people believed to be attending church there was about 14,000 which seems incredible. On Sunday a third of the people attended church wearing white traditional clothing with a Bible in their hand. In the same way, there was the northern city of JeongJu (정주 定州) where almost everyone among its 20,000 citizens attended church. In other words, the attack of the Japanese army and the explosion of Christianity were two of the biggest historical events of that time on the Korean peninsula. The first protestant church was mainly in the northern area of the Korean peninsula.

Some people say this kind of religious movement is because of the oppression of the Japanese army, the progression of the colonization by Japan, and the Russo-Japanese war. In other words, these were sociological factors. However, even though I am not denying there were some kinds of sociological factors, to me this occurred for purely religious reasons. The reason I am thinking this is there are many historical instances around the world of these kinds of hardships yet Christianity did not always flourish there. From the view of Christians, this exactly happened because of God's will. If there was no dangerous political change, PyeongYang would still surely be the center of Christianity in Asia.

Section 5: Tragedy hits the Korean peninsula

For a people who greatly regarded politeness, having a strong relationship with their family and relatives, high morality, and believed that the poor Jesus Christ who was crucified on the cross is the real God, what would come from this? The result is like the sparkling brightness of the frost upon the trees of a snowy mountainside.

An JungGeun (안중근 安重根)

In 1909, the year before the JoSeon dynasty collapsed, at the present day provincial capitol city of Ha El Bin (哈爾賓 Harbin) of the Hei Long Jiang province, An JungGeun, used a pistol from 2 meters away to assassinate Ito Hirobumi, (伊藤博文) the President of the Privy Council of the Japanese government during the movement of Japan to colonize Korea. An JungGeun was the son of a high ranking YangBan Korean official and the leader of a military unit of the underground loyal army (연합대한의군참모중장 連合大韓義軍参謀中将 – "United Alliance Loyal Army Lieutenant General"). He was arrested at that place and after a trial that lasted 6 months was executed the next year.

Every Korean knows while he was in jail he splendidly mirrored the actions of a Japanese Samurai. He was seen as an assassin in Japan, but in Korea he was seen as a loyalist of the underground resistance army. Today there is a memorial house commemorating his act on a hill in Seoul in Nam San Park. He was a follower of Confucianism and a Catholic convert.

There are many writings from him that exist which he wrote during the lengthy trial which lasted more than 5 months. Most of them exist in the form of HanSi (한시 漢詩 : Poems written in Chinese characters) and the contents of them are mostly about promoting friendship between Japan and Korea and that both countries needed to come to know each other. Today these words are still very fitting. Just before his execution, he took a pen and wrote in one stroke these words "Wi-guk-heon-shin goon-in-bon-boon" (위국헌신 군인본분 為国献身 軍人本分 : giving my life for my country is the duty for a soldier).

In 1910, the year An JungGeun was executed, after all, the Korean peninsula was forced to fall under the rule of Japan and the JoSeon Dynasty closed the curtain on a history of 519 years.

The Japanese government put into place a Governor General's Office in Seoul and established Martial Law. Martial Law is rule by a system of military police, so it is easy to understand this being called being ruled by a troop of the Japanese Army's military police stationed on the Korean Peninsula. In other words, these are not policemen but soldiers. 77 separate groups of Japanese soldiers were stationed throughout every district of the Korean peninsula by the Japanese government, and it included 3,410 soldiers. More military police were added, and they ruled the Korean peninsula. Of course, besides the military police, regular Japanese soldiers were also stationed there. To those people who lived on the peninsula, it was the first experience of being ruled by foreigners. It was hard to even imagine this happening for those gentlemen of the East.

One after another regular Japanese citizens also entered Korea from Japan. Among those there were some people who could live well with Koreans or could even be respected by them. However, their relationship was one of a ruler and ruled. The people who could understand the mind of the Koreans well were those Koreans who lived on the Korean peninsula. To the followers of Confucianism and the Sinocentric system the thinking was why should we submit to these people from remote islands floating in the East Sea? More and more life grew harder, and many families became separated from each other.

Arirang, Arirang, Arariyo,

Go over the Pass on Arirang Mountain

There are 12 stages to the passes of Arirang Mountain

This moment is passing through the last stage

Arirang is the mountain of sadness

The road there is a path that has no return

Arirang, Arirang Arariyo,

Go over the Pass on Arirang Mountain

For those people who lived on the Korean peninsula, they had been under the harsh rule of the JoSeon Dynasty, but after that rule ended the situation became worse as they were now being ruled by foreigners.

Independence movement of March 1ˢᵗ

The time from the process of their own country collapsing to being ruled by Japan through colonization was very short, and those people who lived on the Korean peninsula didn't think that this kind of bad dream could last for very long. People started to take action for ridding themselves of the humiliation that had accumulated in their mind. What can be done for standing against the forcible rule of the Japanese government? There was only one way: they had to bring a suit in international society claiming that they were an unarmed country which was attacked and forcibly enslaved. However, the Japanese government had no reason to allow this kind of movement. Those Koreans who had escaped or went to study abroad tried to make the proclamation to sway international opinion. Those Koreans decided to make formal declarations of independence and appeal to the world for help.

In 1919 (the 8th year of Taisho Era), 9 years after the Japanese colonization began, at the Korean YMCA assembly hall in Tokyo Kanda, Korean students read aloud this Korean Declaration of Independence. Presently, there is a monument and an archive room in that assembly hall memorializing that act. In their own country, step by step, preparations were being made to make their own public reading of the Korean Declaration of Independence, but this grew from the resistance that took place first in Japan. On the Korean peninsula, Christians, Cheondoists (천도교 天道教 : followers of Cheondoism which literally means "Religion of the Heavenly Way") Buddhists, and followers of other religions prepared a simultaneous protest across the country. Cheondogyo was started in the last part of the 19th century by Choe JaeWoo (최재우 崔済愚 1824-1864), and it united Confucianism, Buddhism, Taoism, and folk beliefs to make up a Korean national religion. The reason religious people gathered and started this movement is because all Korean political groups had previously been disbanded by the Japanese government. The preparation was accomplished in complete secrecy.

The Korean Declaration of Independence begins: "We herewith proclaim the independence of Korea and the liberty of the Korean people. This we proclaim to all the nations of the world in witness of human equality. This we proclaim to our descendants so that they may enjoy in perpetuity their inherent right to nationhood..." and proclaimed the freedom and equality of the races. Beneath this paragraph was an attachment that proclaimed this was a peaceful movement. At the end of the document the 33 names of the nationalists who prepared it were signed. Among those, 16 were Christians, 15 were Cheondoists, and 2 were Buddhist.

In the early morning of March 1st, secretly they sent the documents to others across the country, and began a simultaneous protest. In the capital city Seoul a copy of the document was handed door to door to every family, and there was a gathering at Pagoda Park (present day TapGol Park), student delegates read the documents aloud and started to walk in a demonstration while shouting "DaeHan DongNip ManSe" (대한독립만세 大韓独立万歳 : Long Live Korean Independence). The Japanese government did not foresee this at all. At the same moment, hundreds of thousands of citizens joined in on this protest.

This demonstration lasted for about 3 months across the country, even though the Japanese Army quickly began attempting to suppress the demonstrators by force. However the people kept shouting "DongNip ManSe" and continued protesting in the face of the Japanese guns. For this reason the Independence Movement of March 1st is also called the Manse Movement. Meeting places numbered 1542 and included an attendance total of more than 2,020,000. The number of killed was 7,509. It was not only a Christian movement but included all Korean people, yet churches were used as meeting places and the church infrastructure was used to spread the word about the protests.

The Korean Joan of Arc – Yoo GwanSoon (유관순 柳寛順)

There are many episodes stemming from the March 1st Movement.

Yoo GwanSoon was a student of Ewha HakDang (이화학당 梨花学堂 : a girls' school) and was 16 years old. Because the school was closed after the March 1st Independent movement, she returned to her hometown where her father along with other believers had built a church. She went up to the mountains to pray "Oh, my Lord, please give me power like Joan of Arc who at age 19 in France fought and won victory for her country." Yoo GwanSoon heard a voice from heaven that said, "GwanSoon, I will give power to you."

After that, she went to the market place and gave out small TaeGeok-Gi (태극기 太極旗 : Korean national flags), made a speech, began to shout out "DongNip ManSe", and led a demonstration march of protest around the square. She believed if a girl was in the front row that they would not be fired upon. Nonetheless, the Japanese military police attacked without discretion, and about 30 people including her parents were killed for their country. She and her brother were arrested, and she was tortured to death in the jail. An innocent girl's death of one who had been raised in a Christian home with an education based in Christianity is still talked about as part of the March 1st Independence Movement. This story appears in elementary school textbooks, and there is no one in Korea today who doesn't know the name of Yoo GwanSoon, the Korean Joan of Arc. How many Japanese would know about this historic fact?

A village destroyed because they believed in Jesus

After the independence movement began, the Japanese Governor General of the Occupying Forces started to persecute the Korean churches. 45 days after that day of March 1st, a tragic incident occurred. There is a village called JeAm-Ri, which is 20 kilometers south, southwest of SooWon City which is located 60 kilometers south of Seoul. The village was the only one in the area and was surrounded by nothing but rice fields. There were 33 houses clustered together all having thatched roofs made from rice stalks. In the middle there still stood a small Methodist church made in the same manner as the people's houses with a thatched roof of rice stalks.

That day, the 15th of April, in the afternoon a Japanese military force, a platoon of about 30 soldiers, entered the village, gathered all of the male residents into the small church, closed the door and windows, poured gasoline, lit it on fire, and shot those who fled the burning building. It happened so suddenly, and some people tried to flee and were shot. Outside, a young newlywed, realized her husband was in the building and tried to run from her house to his aid, but was beheaded by one of the soldiers. A young father who innocently came to church with his newborn baby because the order to gather came so quickly begged for his baby's life and tried to hand the baby to someone outside the church through a window, but both were shot and killed. 23 people died in the massacre. In this village, 6 Cheondoists were also killed nearby, so in total 29 people were sacrificed. Furthermore, all of the houses in the village were set on fire and burned to the ground. Later this village was called "The village destroyed because they believed in Jesus".

This incident happened in retaliation as a demonstration of power by the Japanese government for the independence movement. A Canadian medical missionary, Frank Schofield, who went there one or two weeks after this incident, reported to the New York Times that the unchanged, cruel scenery still remained, and this news went out all over the world. Of course, that news was not reported to the Japanese public. Still in Japan, there are none who know the details of this incident beyond a small few. Japanese reporters were forbidden to enter that area.

In the middle of Seoul City in TapGol Park, the place where the independence movement first gathered, there is a memorial relief of a small baby being passed through a window. In present days, March 1st is a national holiday as the Memorial Day for the beginning of the independence movement.

A housewife named Jeon DongNye (전동례 田同礼), who lost her husband in the JeAm-Ri massacre and continued to live there, said:

After we gained independence, a well-meaning Japanese person visited and humbly apologized to me, but there is a big difference between forgiveness and forgetting. I have been a widow since I was 23 years old, and not a single day has passed where I have not thought of that day up until now when I am 86 years old (in 1982). I will never forget the nightmare of that day till I die and go to heaven to meet my husband again. Still today there are grains of rice which were blackened by the fire of that day which I find when digging in the corner of my garden to plant vegetables. (8)

This protest and move for independence was slowly put down by force by the rigid control of the Japanese Army. However, these stories which I have told about the March 1st Independence movement are in elementary school students' textbooks in Korea and are recounted very clearly.

After the March 1st, 1919 Independence Movement, the Korean peninsula began to fall further into a deep, horrid darkness.

The roaming of "white-clothed people (백의민족 白衣民族)"

Already 40% of the tillable land was handed over to the Japanese, and from the 1930s the Korean peninsula was regarded as a Japanese army supply base for attacking the Chinese continent. Rice was taken by force and sent to the islands of the Japanese archipelago. The people on the Korean peninsula could barely survive on beans, millet, and miscellaneous cereals. Even though the Korean people remained a proud race of people, there was no way to escape from this poor life. The people who had lost their tillable land couldn't even get food, and escaped into the mountains and barely could get enough food to keep from starving to death. Others roamed as far as Siberia, Manchuria, American, Hawaii or Japan in search of food.

On the Korean peninsula from times of old, while women wore colorful Chima-Jeogori (치마 저고리), men usually wore pure white clothing regardless of their social status between being YangBan or normal citizens. Traditional clothing of Confucianism was white clothing which represented their cleanliness, humbleness, innocence, and frugal character. For this reason Koreans were sometimes called "white-clothed people", yet almost 2,500,000 of the white-clothed people ended up being among those who went roaming abroad.

Arirang, Arirang, Arariyo,

Go over the Pass on Arirang Mountain

Does the sun that is going down on the western side mountain go down by its own wish?

Did my dear one who left me here alone leave because of their own desire? (The lyric is from the best known version of the song Arirang.)

Japanese teachers wore swords and forbid their students to use Korean language and taught only in Japanese. If someone used Korean accidentally in the school, they were punished. The people on the Korean peninsula were essentially slaves to the Japanese. Language is the foundation of the culture of a country, so even though you are trying to force change to another language, it is not working out. How could the Japanese government do such a reckless thing at that time? If I think about that for now, the Japanese Military government which started to fight in the Pacific War was unreasonable about many different things.

On the Korean peninsula 137 Shinto shrines were built. Of course at the schools, but also to normal citizens, it was required to worship at the Shinto Shrine and to fly the Hi-no maru (日の丸 : Literally the "Rising

Sun" flag, the Japanese National Flag). This should not have been done this way, but the governor of the Japanese Christian Association went to Korea and persuaded Korean Christians to worship at Shinto Shrines by saying that Shintoism is not a religion. In this manner, the Japanese church assaulted Korean Christians and sinned against them in an unforgivable way.

That famous PyeongYang Seminary which was producing Korean pastors had been closed along with about 200 churches in 1938. About 2,000 believers were imprisoned, and 500 people were martyred.(9)

In 1940, the Japanese government changed the names of all Koreans to Japanese-styled names. For example, at the well-known Ewha Women's University which had a long history, graduates names were listed only in their Japanese form for the remaining duration of the colonization. When viewing that list which today spans more than one hundred years, only the named individuals can recognize themselves among that portion of the list because there are no Korean names registered there. In present day Korea there is a lot of damage which occurred during that period still remaining even in their daily life.

Umesao Tadao (梅棹忠夫), who later became a folklorist, at that time was around 20 years old, said about his experience of visiting the Korean peninsula for his research:

Precisely at the time I was travelling around the countryside on the Korean peninsula. When I entered a village, there were many names posted on bulletin boards of those whose names had just been changed to Japanese form. In the mind of one of my very close Korean friends, this was a very hateful memory. This policy of trying to assimilate 10s of millions of Koreans who had such a high culture into Japanese culture was absurd.(10)

What made the Japanese government do such a horrendous thing?

The Japanese Military Government forced Christians of Korea to bow during Sunday chapel in the direction of the Japanese emperor who lived in the Imperial Palace, placed a household Shinto altar of "Amaterasu Omikami (天照大神)" in the church, cut out some parts of the Bible, and to worship in the Shinto shrines.

One day in a field where a family was planting crops some Japanese soldiers arrived by truck. The parents yelled to their daughter to run away and hide. However that daughter was caught while trying to run away through the field and placed onto the truck and disappeared. Her parents never saw her face again. She was forced to be a "comfort woman" to the military (now admittedly a sex slave) and eventually died there in that service.

Sometimes a human being can be like a devil. The Bible says that it is because evil spirits who serve Satan can enter the bodies of humans and cause them to do the most unimaginable of evil acts. According to the Bible, humans have Original Sin (Adam's sin). The only thing that can free people from this Original Sin is the blood of Christ from the cross. Blood is life, the most valuable treasure on the earth which is worth more than gold or diamonds, the only thing that can make atonement for this sin in the end. Moreover, Christ's blood is God's blood so it can make atonement for every single sin of mankind. During the Japanese colonization era, Christians on the Korean peninsula endured this persecution with their belief in the Cross, waiting for that day of salvation while they were imprisoned. The population of Christians in Korea at that time still only consisted of 1 or 2% of the total population. At the time during the last of the war in 1944, the Japanese government adopted a conscription system on the Korean peninsula too. Those Koreans were sent as Japanese soldiers to the battle lines from the Aleutians and Vladivostok to the South Pacific islands and Burma. Some of them belonged to the suicide squads. 10% of the population of Korea at the time, about 2,000,000 people, was drafted as either soldiers or military support staff. The deep depression of the people who lived at this time is described in the following passage from scholar Ham SeokHeon:

There was not a person who held their newborn baby on their lap who would be forced to grow up under the Japanese Imperial Colonization who would not sigh and think "I have created another life that will only live as a slave. What kind of fate awaits you ...?" If you think about a child's usual pride in their father, to the father who knows the cruel truth that this child would be raised to be a slave, and he should not be bringing a child into this kind of world and still did, this is a very sad fact of life.(11)

On the islands of Japan on June 26, 1942, under suspicion of breaking the Peace Preservation Law, pastors who belonged to the Holiness Church, which was a sect under the Japanese Protestant church, were arrested simultaneously under the charges of not worshipping the Japanese Emperor as God. 350 churches were dissolved and 6 of the imprisoned pastors died in the jail. Furthermore, some of the pastors cooperated with the authorities and helped in the arrest of the others.

During the darkness of these 36 years (1910-1945), almost all Japanese churches had a spirited revival called "Taisho Revival" and "Showa Revival". Nakada Shigeharu (中田重治), Yamamuro Gunpei (山室軍平), and Kagawa Toyohiko (賀川豊彦) were among those who were very active at the time. In other words, at the same time the Korean churches were suffering cruel persecution, the Japanese churches were experiencing a great spiritual movement. Some people such as Uchimura Kanzo (内村鑑三) told the truth and suffered difficult times, but mostly those outspoken people were pushed into the corner of Japanese churches.

A soft voice for singing hymns

I will introduce a beautiful episode which occurred at the first of these dark times

This story comes from the book titled "The Christ of the Korean Heart" which was written by Arch Campbell, an American Protestant missionary:

It happened on an achingly cold night in December when I was in a village on a mountainside in the northern part of Korea. While walking along a small path bordered by small shops, one of the doors which were made of old, cracked paper, leaked a small yellow light into the street. I could hear a melody being sung by a small, hushed voice coming from that house where a family sat in a small circle.

"Yesu, Yesu, kuihan Yesu ... (예수 예수, 귀한 예수... *Jesus, Jesus, precious Jesus ...)"*

It must be family worship time. All around Korea there was this kind of poor family sitting together on the OnDol (warmed floor) before going to bed. Suddenly I was reminded of my hometown in America. My heart was warmed with the memories of my own home on the hill.(12).

All Korean people surely know there are these kinds of families living around them even though the numbers were not many. From this kind of Christian home, sometimes came people as a bright light like the Korean Joan of Arc.

Martyrs blood became the seed

If you think about it clearly, Korean churches were always under persecution from 1784 for the Catholic church and 1884 for the Protestant church until the Pacific War finished (1945). There was not even a single peaceful moment during that time. For that long time, churches endured and survived. Supporting them were the words of the scriptures from the Bible:

He who finds his life will lose it, and he who loses his life for My sake will find it. (Matthew 10:39)

When He had called the people to *Himself*, with His disciples also, He said to them, "Whoever desires to come after Me, let him deny himself, and take up his cross and follow Me. (Mark 8:34)

People were watching the Christians. It looked on the surface like the numbers of Christians were not increasing much, but beneath the surface there was a desperate calling that was burning like magma. This point cannot be denied that after World War II, the explosion of Christian believers in Korea resulted from the widespread respect of people for those Catholic and Protestant believers who had endured through this persecution. This is exactly the proof of the martyrs' blood being the seed as Tertullianus said.

Chapter 2 - Ethnicity character and Christian belief

Section 1 The people who escaped to the south

Independence for a short time

The dark times ended on August 15, 1945 with the defeat of the Japanese army. This day is called "GwangBok-Jeol (광복절 光復節)" which means "the independence day which recovered the light" and is celebrated as a national holiday.

Japanese and Koreans who had cooperated with the Japanese army didn't have any place left to stand and were viewed coldly, sworn at, and had objects thrown at them. All over Korea, Koreans organized groups called "preservation committees" who worked to save the peace and prevent anarchy, and about 900,000 Japanese who had been on the Korean peninsula were sent.

On the other hand, around 1,500,000 of the 2,000,000 Koreans forced to go to Japan returned to Korea from across the sea. Around 600,000 people who for a variety of reasons couldn't return to Korea remained in Japan. In other words, the negative effects of the colonization era didn't end then as those who had to remain in Japan and their descendants still live under unfair conditions. When I say under unfair conditions, it means those who were forced to become Japanese citizens were then once again returned to being foreigners, and from that time lived in Japan but are now living in Japan as Koreans (재일한국인/조선인 在日韓国人・朝鮮人) and paying taxes but with limited citizenship rights. A Korean Christian Church in Japan church which had been near my house was a place where these people

60

gathered. There are some Japanese who say to them "if you are unhappy about something, you can become naturalized Japanese citizens". However, they are hiding their tears and answering like this, "There is not even a single word of apology, and that easily you say to just become a naturalized citizen. You are not treating us as humans." A person who becomes a naturalized citizen is as important a decision as that of getting married, but Japanese people do not seem to understand the importance and gravity of making such a decision.

The people on the Korean peninsula had everything taken away from them, and they were one of the poorest countries in the world. However they were very happy about their independence and shouted "ManSe!" (Full life!)

There were more than 50 Protestant pastors and church elders who were verbally abused and tortured in prison, withered away to skin and bones, and died, but those who survived were released from prison. In Korean, those survivors are called "ChulOk SeongDo" (출옥성도 出獄聖徒 : Holy people who were released from prison). They severely criticized those pastors and believers who had worshiped in the Shinto shrines and insisted those people should show repentance for a period of 2 months. Those people who had cooperated with the Japanese army were excused as having no other choice under that situation. The gap between these two parties still exists today. Those Christian survivors founded seminaries based on their beliefs and trained their successors. The KoRyeo Seminary in BuSan is one such seminary.

With the surrender of the Japanese, the Korean peninsula was divided at the 38th parallel into South and North and occupied by U.S and U.S.S.R. military respectively. Under the watch of the U.N. the first democratic election was held, and Lee SeungMan (이승만 李承晚) was elected president and established South Korea as an independent country in name and in reality. However, only the south participated in this election without the North. The North side chose to move forward as a communist country and called their country JoSeon. This name has a very long history. Around 200 BC there was an actual country on the Korean peninsula. The south side which was named "DaeHanMinGuk (대한민국 大韓民国)" was founded in 1948, but it also came from a part of the name of several historical countries called Han (MaHan, JinHan, and ByeonHan 마한, 진한, 변한 馬韓、辰韓、弁韓).

The persecution that occurred in the North

The U.S.S.R. army who occupied the north after the end of the war two months later introduced Kim IlSeong (김일성 金日成 : the grandfather to Kim JeongEun) to the people. He was a general of the north side's army and was announced as the first leader of North Korea which went on to become a communist country. The Christians sensed there was a new danger approaching. That new danger appeared as Kim Ilseong began persecuting the Christians there. Some pastors and church elders were arrested and others just disappeared. There were some pastors though who were able to escape at the very last moment. I want to talk about one of those pastors, Han KyeongJik (한경직 韓景職). You can know about the situation of the time by learning about him.

Han KyoungJik was born in 1902 in a very rural area to an agricultural family in the Northern Province of PyeongAn-Do (평안도 平安道 : "Do" means an area of land slightly larger than a "Ken (県)" in Japan) during the JoSeon Dynasty. When he was 13 years old, he was married to a woman 3 years older than him that was chosen by his parents following the custom of that time. At age 16 he fathered a son. This was at the first of the time Protestant Christian missionaries had begun working in Korea, and his parents were converted to Christianity by the words of the missionaries. In that way, he also was educated as a Christian on his mother's lap from the time he was very young. When he was 23 years old, he graduated from a Christian school in PyeongYang and went to America to study for about 7 years, and when he was 31, he became a formal pastor in a Presbyterian church in the north of Korea. That means the year he became an official pastor was 1933, and this is the harshest time under the era of Japanese colonization.

At the time he became a pastor, there were not many who had the experience of studying abroad. He was a man of moderate views and well-balanced, and although he was young, he was a leader that other people depended upon. Under the rule of the Japanese Military government's severe persecution, he managed to avoid being arrested or imprisoned, but for the final two years prior to the Japanese surrender he was forbidden to preach in the church. At the war's ending, communist persecution of the church began. One autumn day in 1945 just before he was about to be arrested by the new ruling communist army, he was able to escape from danger and ran away by truck, train, and finally on foot to cross the 38th parallel to reach Seoul in the south. Of course there was not enough time to go home and retrieve his family before he fled. Fortunately, later his family also escaped to the south and they were reunited.

In December of 1945 Pastor Han with 27 others who had escaped from the north started a church called Bithynia Mission Church in the YeongNak area of Seoul. At that time the YeongNak area was full of refugees from the north. In the next year, they were told to change the name of the church to reflect the name of the area, so the name was changed to YeongNak Presbyterian Church. There was no building for the church only a tent. Of course there were many Christians among those who had escaped the north, so every Sunday the numbers of attendees increased. In the mornings on Sunday chapel time had to be held twice to accommodate all of them.

Although the people were poor, they made offerings to the church and would go there to work either in the early morning before going to their regular work or on their way back home after finishing work. By their hands they built the largest church in Korea at the time. Furthermore, they opened a middle school and high school to educate the poor children of those families who had escaped from the north. Along the way, on Sunday, June 25th of 1950, the morning service was held as usual, but the afternoon service was filled with a different atmosphere because they heard the news the communist army of the north had suddenly attacked the south. The next day the army reached Seoul City and the day after that on the 27th under bombardment the people fled without time to say goodbye to their families. This was the beginning of the Korean War.

The next year they returned to Seoul City and reunited with their families. However one of the church elders who had tried to protect the church from the communist army had been killed. A church elder means one of those people who is a part of church leadership and is elected for a life term by a 2/3rd majority vote of members. This kind of church who has elders who have all of the responsibility in the church is called Presbyterian church.

After this, Pastor Han worked hard for saving the war orphans and developing more churches, and for the duration of the war the YeongNak church's work continued. From the 1960s to the 1970s there were many difficulties that included poverty, persecution by the military government, problems between Japan and Korea, the student led anti-government demonstrations, and the war in Vietnam. He worked as a leader of the Korean Protestant church and retired at age 70 in 1973. In the following year of 1974 his wife whom he had wed when he was 13 years old died, and he was called to heaven in 2000 at the age of 97.

Pastor Han was a moderate theologian who had studied in Princeton Seminary, and at the same time he was a very practical minded activist. The Presbyterian Church in Korea was basically divided into two groups. One group was conservative and the other was conservative progressive. Pastor Han was the leader of the conservative progressive group. Now in 2012 YeongNak Church is a mega-church. A church with more than 50,000 members attending is called a mega-church.

The Korean War

On the south side in 1949 the Tillable Land Reform Law was enacted the next year, so all farmers had their own land and were independent farmers. Korea, as had happened in Japan, was a country reborn in the modern age. Under this kind of situation, the attack I mentioned before by the communist army struck like a bolt from out of the blue. It was a war between people of the same race, and it was even a war between families and relatives to some people. In response to this, the U.N. defined the North as the aggressor and sent a U.N. army consisting of forces from 16 countries made up mostly of U.S. soldiers to defend the South. This is called the Korean War. Even though that long rule by the Japanese army had barely ended, the entire Korean peninsula became a battlefield. It started June 25th of 1950 and lasted until July of 1953, 3 full years of war. However, the first 9 months were like the confusion that follows a typhoon striking.

The Communist Army marched rapidly into the south and covered 30 kilometers per day. Soon they occupied all of the country except for the edge of the south east side in the BuSan area. As their armed forces marched south, the north side constructed People's Committees along the way to try to establish the entire peninsula as being communist. However, on September 15th, 3 months after the war started, the U.S. Army launched a surprise attack at Incheon, near Seoul. Seoul City became the center of strong fighting with battles in the streets. 50 to 60 percent of the city was completely destroyed. The communist army who had marched further south retreated to the north through the mountains.

At this time the U.N. Army troops chased the Communist troops across the 38th Parallel and pushed them back nearly to the border of China on the northern border. Then the Chinese army joined the communist forces. The U.N. Army started to retreat, and Seoul City was occupied once again by the Communist Army. The U.N. Army reestablished their positions and recovered Seoul again. This all happened during the first 9 months of the war. During this time, too many people and soldiers were sacrificed. At PanMoonJeom (판문점 板門店) at the 38th Parallel peace talks began. While the talks took place, the bombing and fighting continued. Finally on July 27th, 1953, an Armistice agreement was signed to stop the fighting, and this armistice is still in place to this day. Nowadays, South Korean people are still worrying about when the fighting will start again.

The Korean War was a war without a victor, and it still remains that way. Through this war, the north side lost 2,720,000 people which was 28.4% of the northern population. The south side lost 1,330,000 people. The U.S. army dead was as high as 63,000. On this small peninsula dead bodies were piled up like mountains. Most South Korean people still haven't forgotten their debt of thanks to the US for making this great sacrifice even though they were foreigners for defending them against being forced to become communist. Because the Korean War was a material resources superiority war fought with the greatest amount of modern weaponry though not including nuclear weapons, there were massive casualties. It was the literal embodiment of the expression of "scorched earth".

Just as an aside, in Korea this war is called "DongNan" (동란 動乱 : disturbance) or "Yug-Yio" (육이오 6-25, or June 25th the day the war started) because this was a war fought against their own. Koreans suffered unspeakable cruelty on the Korean peninsula with 36 years of colonization, 5 years of separation after that, and then 3 years of civil war following that.

Churches built by those people who came from the north

During the time from when the war was going on and even after the armistice was signed, a lot of people fled the north seeking freedom in spite of the tremendous danger. The number of refugees was as many as 4,000,000 to 4,500,000 people. This was as much as half of the northern population of 9,600,000. Among those who fled were many Christians like I mentioned before such as Pastor Han GyeongJik.

I will introduce another one of them, Pastor Kim Chang in (김창인 金昌仁)

He was born in the north, converted to Christianity along with his parents, became a pastor, and fought against the Japanese Imperialists forcing people to worship at the Shinto Shrines. After gaining freedom from the soldiers of the Japanese Army, when the north was supported by the U.S.S.R. and China and was on the way to becoming a communist country, he fled to Seoul from PyeongYang in search of religious freedom.

On September 6th of 1953 he started the ChungHyeon Presbyterian Church in an area called ChungHyun in Seoul City with 13 other believers who had fled the north together. It was only 2 months after Seoul City was completely burned to the ground from the Korean War. That area was a place which was lined with a market and shops and many people who had escaped from the north were living there.

The specialty of Pastor Kim and the 18 other believers was having the strength of belief of the Christians who had made PyeongYang into the Jerusalem of the East in the early 1900s. All of those believers had direct spiritual experience. This was the foundation of the prosperity of ChungHyeon Presbyterian Church. Spiritual experience is never manifested twice in the same manner. In a different time it is manifested in a different way, but when someone felt this inspired, there would only be one way to express it as having been moved by the Holy Spirit. One who has had this kind of experience can understand this, but others cannot easily understand this. The atmosphere covering all of this area was filled with unwavering strong belief.

In the worship services in ChungHyeon Presbyterian Church, a special atmosphere that could be felt by anyone who visited filled the air, and they surely could believe that God was present. Seeking this kind of worship, those refugees who came from the north attended this church, and the numbers grew from week to week. People felt they were filled with the presence of God through this worship, respected God, and offered their 10% tithes to the church from their small incomes according to the laws of the Old Testament. This kind of passion attracted many others to attend as well. Nowadays in Korea, there are more than a few churches which have a foundation built by those refugees from the north.

The feeling of the presence of the Holy Spirit was not the only special thing. Pastor Kim had suffered from tuberculosis when he was a child, and after he became a pastor still sometimes coughed up blood. However, he kept on giving his sermon even during these attacks. People were greatly moved by his passion and commitment. After that also this church continued to add to their numbers. The numbers grew to the hundreds, then thousands. The church building was also rebuilt many times. Pastor Kim had a big influence on young soldiers in Korea which lived under a strict situation with North Korea, and on April 25th in 1972, 3,473 soldiers were baptized in a single ceremony. To have this many people baptized in a single ceremony is a very rare event in history and surprised the Korean people.

After that in 1983, the number of believers in ChungHyeon Church was over 10,000, and it became a mega-church. Former South Korean President Kim YeongSam (김영삼 金泳三) also is one of the church elders at this church. Those believers who attend this church now are training to be missionaries to the North once unification occurs. I don't have specific statistical information on this church after the 1990s.

I will add another word here to avoid any misunderstanding. Some people say the number of Christian believers who came from the North to the South is the biggest reason that after the war churches have been so strong, but this is not the case. Even though you could say at that time there were a large number of Christian believers in the North, there were only about 2000 churches and about 300,000 believers. Not all of those fled to the south. The percentage of peop e who were Christians was a small amount compared to the total number of those refugees who fled to the south which was as many as 4,000,000 to 4,500,000. The explosion of the Christian population occurs later, and it was a new happening in Korea that started from the inside.

Section 2 – The Darkness passes with a new dawn

With the signing of the Korean Armistice the dark ages on the Korean peninsula were truly finished. However, the beautiful peninsula was now divided into two sides who struggled against each other.

It is not well-known what happened to the churches in North Korea after the division took place. Because the North had become a communist country, the churches there were persecuted in a new way. The situation about the many Christians who had fled to the south I already mentioned before. The story of the Korean peninsula including North Korea is now finished. From now, I will talk only about Christianity in South Korea.

Reconstruction Begins (from 1953)

The people who were displaced returned to their hometowns, and the believers returned to the church. When you think about having been under severe persecution and the country's situation of having been burned to the ground, you cannot expect the data about the Korean Christian population. It was estimated in around 1953 there were about 157,000 Catholic believers and around 600,000 Protestant believers. This is only 3.7% of the total population of 20,700,000 in South Korea at that time.

Because of having come through a long history of martyrdom, the Christian church has earned the trust of the people, so people started to attend church with the coming of peace. Let's look at the situation of the explosion of the Christian population according to political and social change which was almost unprecedented in the history of man. Doing this surely confirms the way in which Korea changed to a

Christian country from being a country of Confucianism. I personally experienced the food shortage in Japan following the war and heard many stories from others who suffered in poverty. Sometimes major incidents occurred. Yet, under these conditions Japan succeeded in recovering economically. The special procurements Japan received for assisting in the Korean War provided good material for the economic recovery. At the time the Korean War started, Japan had already escaped from the worst of their economic situation. On the other hand, Korea suffered from a lack of sufficient food, the destruction of homes, very few chances for employment, and was one of the poorest countries in the world.

There is 8 years difference between the economic development of Japan and Korea, and this is because of when the wars started and finished. (The war in Japan ended in 1945. The war in Korea ended in 1953.) Korea started recovery 8 years later than Japan. If you are someone who has personally experienced this economic recovery in Japan, and you keep in mind this 8 year difference, you can easily understand the process that was taking place in Korea. In other words, it can be said that Korea followed the same steps as Japan to economic recovery.

In 1953 (The 28th year of Showa in Japan) the year of the signing of the Armistice Treaty, Korean people had little food and were in the midst of much suffering. Some of the intellectuals among the people who had remained along with some of those who had fled abroad started to rebuild their country. In 1954 America and Korea signed the U.S./R.O.K. Mutual Security Agreement and America started their support of South Korea. In the same was as Japan had done before, Korea recovered by standing on the foundation of the American support.

Japan and Korea are as similar as brothers in the manner of their progress in politics, economy, and culture and in many other ways. It really seems as though they are twins in this manner of development having been based on Chinese culture and progressing on towards American culture. In regards to the change from the feudalistic age to the modern age, Japan is only one step ahead of Korea and colonized them. The unfair history of Japan treating Korea as inferior without any real justification still heavily influences Japanese thinking, but this is a very hurtful thing for the people of both countries.

Economic development under the Bak JeongHee (박정희 朴正熙) government

The Yi SeungMan government who was in charge of the newly formed South Korea after World War II ended collapsed in 1960 due to student demonstrations which was called the Sa-IlGu (4-19 or April 19th) Revolution. In 1961, under the continuing threat of hostile North Korea, the Bak JeongHee government started with a military coup. Because the Bak JoengHee government tried to rule the country with military power, the critics were divided about him, but one thing that cannot be denied is that he built up the Korean economy. In 1962 the first 5 year economic plan was started, and Korea borrowed money from other countries and took positive steps toward economic development. The policy was to improve the quality of people's lives by increasing exports and it succeeded.

The government tried to assist in the recovery of the economy and move towards modernization by placing young economists who had studied in America in important positions. A key development was in 1965, when Korea established formal diplomatic relations with Japan, and with that influx of foreign capital from Japan planned the route for further economic growth concentrated on exports. Exports increased incredibly with a record 30% average growth each year. However the results of the improvements did not yet reach every corner of Korea, and many people continued to live under difficult conditions. Finally in 1969 entrants to middle school no longer needed to pass entrance exams. Even though they were poor, people now freely had the opportunity to receive education. This means economic development was visibly taking place.

At that same time Japan was experiencing rapid economic growth, the bullet trains started running, the Tokyo Olympics were held in 1964 gathering people from all over the world, and with these kinds of things people everywhere were paying attention to the newborn Japan. Yet in Korea people were still living in deep poverty. If you were to express the Korea of the 1960s in one word, that word would be 'poverty'. In Korea the GDP per capita was only $97 in 1960 (In Japan it was $458), and truly it was one of the poorest countries in the world. Even as late as 1970 the GDP per capita only rose to $254 (In Japan it was $1,895) The percentage of the population involved with agriculture was over 60%. Even though many people entered the cities looking for work, there was no work for them, so people returned to the countryside and just lived with the aid of their family relatives.

The Christian population starts to increase (1960s)

The numbers of Protestants were slowly increasing after the Korean War. In 1960 this number reached about 1,500,000. Still the increase had not yet gotten the attention of other people. However, ten years later in 1970 the numbers had more than doubled and climbed to 3,200,000. Catholic believers also increased by nearly double from 430,000 to 780,000. Both of them added together made up 12.6% of the total Korea population of 32,200,000. The biggest reasons for this rapid growth can be attributed to the absence of persecution and the advent of peaceful times. The number of those who said they had some religious belief was more than 10% of the population which had an influence not only on the religious side but also on the economic and political aspects of the country. However, because Christians had been oppressed and persecuted for such a long time, no one could imagine that Christians would have some influence on society as a whole.

In 1967, 22 years after the end of World War II, the Japan Christian Association made a special proclamation called "The confession of the Japan Christian Association's liability in World War II" to apologize for the sins they committed during the war. That proclamation was made in apology to all the countries of Asia due to the fact the governor of the Japan Protestant Church earlier had gone to the Korean Protestant Church for persuading them to worship in the Shinto shrines. The contents were an apology, but the title was not an "apology" but a "confession of liability" which was a theological title that was not easy to comprehend exactly what was being said and was not an expression of humility. The Korean Christian Church received this calmly, but some Christians were not appeased and claimed the Japanese Christian Church was not admitting to the whole truth about their actions.

A very important event occurred in the late 1960s. In 1969 Korean Archbishop Kim SooHwan (김수환 金寿煥) was selected as a Cardinal in the Catholic Church. Being selected as a Cardinal means he was a leader of the entire Catholic Church and that in the future the possibility existed for him to be selected as Pope of the Roman Catholic Church. This was inspiring news to Koreans who had suffered under the confusion and poverty that followed the Korean War. For example it is the same as in Japan when Dr. Hideki Yukawa (湯川秀樹) was awarded a Nobel Prize which gave hope and pride to Japanese people who were living in the dark times following World War II. As the church began to progress, the Korean economy and society began to rapidly progress.

Why Christians diligently spread the gospel

Before I say more about other things, here I want to explain about Christian missionaries. Why do Christians diligently spread the gospel?

The people who believe in Jesus Christ want to spread their happiness to others because of their gratitude for being saved. However, after being persecuted or imprisoned for 30 or 40 years, the desire of missionaries might be reduced. Under persecution it might happen that those who received the gospel might be put in danger. Even though this was the case, why did Christians spread the gospel?

The truth is that the work of Christian missionaries was not by their own will, but if you examine the fact carefully, it was by the commandment of Jesus Christ to go and spread the gospel. That commandment is according to the following scripture:

Go, then, to all people everywhere and make them my disciples: baptize them in the name of the Father, the Son, and the Holy Spirit, and teach them to obey everything I have commanded. (Matthew 28:19-20)

This was written as an order, an imperative sentence. If this commandment did not exist, Christianity would not be spread all over the world. The reason is that even though you are a Christian, you would lose your strength for doing missionary work while you suffer under hard times or persecution, and without anyone noticing there would be a reduction in the number of people who spread the gospel of Christianity. In the end, Christianity itself might not even exist in the world today.

However, Korean Christians continued spreading the gospel even under the persecution of the JoSeon Dynasty, the Japanese Imperial Rule, and experiencing the Korean War. This is because the work of a missionary is by Christ's commandment. Of course this is not only because of Christ's commandment but also because of their personal desires stemming from their grateful hearts which believed Jesus Christ died on the cross for them.

Furthermore, there are several other passages in the Bible encouraging Christians to be missionaries of the church.

> ... I solemnly urge you to preach the message, to insist upon proclaiming it (whether the time is right or not), to combine, reproach, and encourage, as you teach with all patience. (2nd Timothy 4:1-2)

> Let those who wept as they planted their crops, gather the harvest with joy! (Psalms 126:5)

The reason the numbers of Christians increased rapidly after World War II was because Christians tried hard to spread the gospel which I will talk about more now, but before that, Christ's commandment to go and spread the word was the first reason. Without this commandment, it might happen that Christianity would not be anywhere in the world, including Korea. If you consider the history of the world, as I quoted from the book of Matthew before the commandment from Christ to *"Go, then, to all people everywhere and make them my disciples"* (Matthew 28:19) is a very important passage, but it is not easy to understand the total importance even if you are a historian. Still, with the concept that Korean Christianity also started from this passage in mind, read the following stories I will share.

The bonds of family and missionaries

There was a kind, young man in his late 20s. He was working in a factory on the outskirts of Seoul City, and when lunch break had nearly finished a lady greeted him, "Annyeonghaseyo" (안녕하세요:Good afternoon). After that, every day at the same time that lady approached the young man and inquired of him, "Won't you go to church?" He answered, "I am not going." However, this continued for about a month. According to Japanese custom, coming every day to keep inquiring is an almost unheard of event. It might result in criminal charges for stalking. But in Korean custom it is only a persistent person who believes something is good, so it is not so uncommon. Their relationships are doggedly deep, so it might not be seen as bothersome to Koreans. Or it might be an aspect of continental character which is not affected as much by such events and is much more magnanimous. That young man just answered "I am not going" because he did not want to go.

One day, that lady said, "Come only one time just as a favor to me." The young man answered, "Okay, I will go only once." In the church there was an atmosphere of acceptance for this kind of young man and a system was in place as well. He was welcomed into the church by many people and the pastor also asked him to attend a Bible study for beginners. If you go once, that will become twice, and then the chance of becoming a regular is highly likely. This kind of example is a very common thing in Korean society.

If a mother asks this of her children or a wife asks her husband, the percentage would be even higher. Korean pastors are especially expecting for wives to inquire of their husbands. At first, a husband will answer, "I am not going." But if she continues to inquire, he will answer, "Okay, only one time." And that is almost the same as saying, "I am following you." They say that in this way, several years later, the husband will be more passionate than his wife.

Being lead to be a believer by a partner or a family member is one of the reasons of the explosion of growth of Korean Christians. In Japan and Korea there is high likelihood the husband will simply refuse to go to church when invited. However, in Korea there is a good chance that if the wife persistently inquires of the husband in the end the husband will follow the will of the wife while Japanese husbands mostly continue to obstinately refuse. What causes the difference between these two? Korean husbands have in their ethnic character to accept things if there is reasonable cause. However it might be that Japanese husbands cannot forgive themselves or in order to save face do not want to accept even though there is a reasonable cause or there is logic in the words of their wife once they have made a decision.

It might be that most Japanese are thinking Korea is a country of Confucianism, so men have more power than women more than in Japan, but the truth is that in the home the women have more power than the men. Outside of the home, a wife stands behind her husband. In the home the wife leads the house well. It looks like continuing to refuse the wife is truly difficult.

This is usually also the same case between close relatives. In Korea there is a saying that "close relatives are family" and when Christian relatives make requests of them there is a good possibility they will follow. As I said, one of the reasons for the explosion of Christianity in Korea is due to family invitations. However, as you will see, this is not the only reason for its occurrence. There are also many other factors that came together and resulted in this taking place.

Korean pastors

Besides regular Sunday morning services, every morning at 4 or 5 o'clock Korean pastors have to wake up, go to church, hold morning service (the Protestant Church calls this service as "Gido Hwe" (기도회 祈祷会 : Prayer Meeting), and deliver sermons to 10s, 100s, or in large churches, more than 10s of thousands attendants. In Korea, Protestant Churches traditionally hold Wednesday evening services that are the same as Sunday afternoon services (these are also called "Gido Hwe").

On Friday night, they hold "Cheolya Gido Hwe" (철야기도회 徹夜祈祷会 : Overnight). Every one of these "Gido Hwe" services also include the pastor speaking for about 30 minutes. It depends on the size of the church, but there are usually several pastors in each church, and the work is divided among them. However, pastors are working on sermons, speeches, counseling, committee meetings, funeral ceremonies, wedding ceremonies and other assorted church tasks from 4AM until 9 or 10PM. Pastors are working so hard that church members think there is no time for them to sleep.

I know about the life of American or European pastors, but I have never seen anyone work harder than Korean pastors. Korean pastors are truly diligent, industrious, and passionate. This reminds me of the image of diligence from the followers of Confucianism of the JoSeon dynasty who woke up very early in the morning, took ritual baths, and read Chinese classic books. Korea's climate and unique history influenced the expansion of Christianity, too. When I was just starting to research the Korean church, I could feel the big influence of Confucianism in church activities, and as time passed, I could feel more of the underlying effect of the influence of climate and ethnicity. In my opinion, this ethnicity means Koreans' pureness. I will cover this more specifically later.

Section 3 — Love your God and love your neighbor

In Christianity besides "go and spread My word" there is another important passage which is the commandment (teaching) of Love as "love your God and love your neighbor". This passage is from the Bible, and when a scholar of the Old Testament asked Christ which was the most important rule He answered in this way:

> Jesus said to him, "'You shall love the Lord your God with all your heart, with all your soul, and with all your mind.' "This is the first and great commandment. "And the second is like it: 'You shall love your neighbor as yourself'. (Matthew 22:37-39)

Love as God's commandment

In Christianity loving your God is a higher priority than loving your neighbor. The reason is if there is no God, there would be no human created and no human beings living in this world. In everything, God is coming first and following this commandment is Christianity. Standing on this foundation, you have to love your neighbor. This commandment of love is in the form of an imperative sentence. In the Bible, God's commandments are without exception in the form of an imperative sentence. It is not okay to keep or not keep. Orders surely must be kept. This commandment of "Love of neighbors" is also the same way.

In Japan before implementing a welfare system, not only pastors, Fathers, Sisters and Christian believers, but also Buddhist monks and followers were taking care of orphans and the poor. Furthermore they

cared for those suffering from leprosy and tuberculosis. Upon entering
the 1990s the Korean government finally began a social welfare system,
but prior to this under the difficult history which I mentioned before,
Christians cared for the poor and suffering under almost every condition
even though they were also poor and suffering under persecution. In
Korea the first western medicine hospital was named 「GwangHye-Won"

(광혜원 広恵院). In 1885 the Presbyterian Church's first medical
missionary Horace Allen who I mentioned before opened this hospital.
Nowadays this is Severance Hospital located beside YeonSe University in
Seoul. After that many hospitals and clinics were opened by Christian
doctors. Following that, Seoul National University Hospital and
corporate hospitals were opened. In other words, that means that in
the case of welfare and medical care Christians played a very important
role. The background of this is Christ's commandment of love.

The commandment of love which Christ taught is unconditional love
which doesn't ask for anything in return. Someone who acts on this
commandment of love doesn't think to consider if I do this it will reflect
well on Christians and will be a benefit to the missionaries. They acted
in a pure way to do what Jesus had taught. I think Korean people had a
good opinion of Christianity as a religion with Christians doing their
work in this manner for decades without seeking public recognition. It
might be that the action of giving unconditional love would not have
continued in the face of many difficulties if Christ had not been crucified
on the cross and sacrificed himself and hadn't taught the
commandment of love. Now you can understand why the teachings of
the Bible were usually taught as imperative sentences.

Nowadays 80% of welfare facilities in Korea were started by Christians
and the remaining 20% are public facilities. If I speak more specifically,
in 2009 there are 1218 Catholic facilities and 553 Protestant facilities.
Furthermore Protestant Churches have 11 foundations from across their
sects for providing assistance. Government support started in 1990, and
from now instituted a countrywide welfare system, so there would be a
larger percentage of public funded welfare projects. However, up until

this moment the Fathers, Sisters, Pastors, and Christian members have played a very important role.

Actual practice of love – the case of Pastor Son YangWon (손양원 孫良源)

A man named Son YangWon was born in 1902. When he was 7 years old, his parents converted to Christianity, so he also believed in Christianity. While under the Japanese Imperial Rule, he was expelled from his elementary and middle school because he refused to worship at the Shinto Shrine. When he was 19 years old, he came to Japan and studied English literature in Waseda University. However, when he was 21 years old he experienced the Holy Spirit and returned to Korea and entered PyeongYang Seminary. Then when he was 30 years old he graduated and became a pastor. In 1940 he was arrested for not worshiping at the Shinto Shrine and imprisoned for 5 years. In 1945 he was released from prison with the finishing of the war and moved to the south side of Korea and lived. While he was working as a pastor in a church, he was affectionately caring for leprosy sufferers. In 1948 before North Korea had attacked, a riot took place. His two sons were shot and killed by a communist party member.

The killer was a young man named An JaeSeon (안재선). Pastor Son submitted a written petition to reduce the punishment for him, and after An JaeSeon was released from jail, Pastor Son adopted and cared for him in the place of his two sons who had died. In 1950, Pastor Son was working to maintain his church while the Korean War was going on and was attacked by communist soldiers and killed when he was 48 years old. Pastor Son's life was a great inspiration to many people. In Korea, people call him "atomic bomb of love". Even though it was called atomic bomb, his atomic bomb was filled with love and moved many people.

I will introduce another impressive story that I heard before.

There was another young man in Korea who was relatively richer than others and each month was receiving what amounted to about 5000 Yen in Japanese money from his father. He stopped smoking and gave up drinking alcohol after becoming a Christian. He thought 1000 Yen a month was enough for him, so he donated the remaining 4000 Yen per month to help support poor students to continue their studies. He continued doing this for 10 years. Later he became a pastor and set off on assignment for his work to an island. On the island he adopted and raised 3 orphans along with his own 2 children. At first he was going to raise only one orphan, but by chance the boy he had chosen had two brothers. Feeling it would be a shame to separate the brothers, he adopted the three boys together.

In Korea there are many similar stories which have moved people. This comes from the commandment in Christianity to love your neighbors as yourself. Korean people began to hear many of these kinds of stories of Christian selfless acts, and these became a grassroots movement for growing Christianity. This was in the 1960s.

Mission Schools in Korea

Mission schools in Japan focused on common education the same as public schools, but mission schools in Korea focused on Bible education. This is a marked difference between the mission schools for Japan and Korea. This is because Korean mission schools thought that true education started from when a person became a Christian and became a new being.

In Korea, some pastors teach that before a person is baptized they need to introduce at least one new person to the church. This is because a person who did not do this is thought to not have enough belief in God. Most of the pastors who are working in the schools have strong convictions about educating missionaries. In Korea, church and mission schools have a strong bond for working for developing missionaries.

The first modern education facility in Korea was BaeJae HakDang (배재학당 培材学堂) which was founded in 1885. HakDang means elementary school in Japan, and it was the first education facility for increasing the overall literacy rate. At that time, Korean society did not rate very highly Christian schools which had just been established. However, missionaries started to build schools at the same time as they started churches.

Those schools built by missionaries were very small at first, but later they slowly became bigger. The Presbyterian Church first built an orphanage which later became present-day YeonSe University. Nowadays, Ehwa Women's University was built by Lady Mary F. Scranton, the mother of the first Methodist missionary. She opened that school for a single, poor student under her care. Like this there are many cases of churches opening schools for orphans or children whose parents were too poor to provide for them. These kinds of schools nowadays have become very famous schools or hospitals in Korea.

Especially in the case of women's education, the Christian church has played a large role. For Korean society to become modernized, the education of women provided by the Christian church and mission schools was substantial. During the Joseon Dynasty there was almost no chance for women to be educated, and it was even considered as a virtue for women to not have much knowledge of the world. Even though women were powerful within the family unit and in the home, their leadership was not accepted in the outside world and authority usually belonged to the men. Surely you can say the independence of women in Korea can be traced to the church and mission schools. Until recently in society, most of the women leaders were graduates of Christian schools.

Bible schools all over the country

Every region in Korea opened schools for Bible studies separately from mission schools. This is another differentiating fact between Korea and Japan. These Bible schools educated people who were leaders in the church. Additionally, many seminaries were opened which were training pastors. After World War II most of these kinds of Bible schools or seminaries became colleges and furthermore became universities. There are many famous Christian universities such as YeonSe University, Ewha University, and SeoGang University. Due to this kind of history, most Christian colleges and universities place heavy emphasis on Bible study in their curriculum. Students also actively participate in various Bible related courses. The atmosphere is very different from mission schools in Japan.

In other words, in Korea mission schools were opened for people who couldn't read, the poor, or women, but in Japan, seminaries were opened as just another school among various schools. However, up until World War II opening a college or university in Korea was forbidden, so there was no other choice than to go abroad to Japan or America for advanced education.

At this time in 2009 in Korea, there are 177 Protestant related high schools with enrollments totaling more than 180,000 students, 41 universities and 25 colleges for a total of 66 with total enrollments of about 370,000 students. Lately public schools have increased, but in modern Korea if you say 'school' it almost always means 'Christian related' school. This is another factor in the explosion in the numbers of Christians in Korea after World War II. Nowadays the numbers of students have been reduced by the decrease in population due to the declining birthrate.

Section 4 – Korean ethnic character: pureness

An on the spot survey of churches in Korea --- the difficulty of collecting data

I conducted an on the spot survey of churches in Korea for 2 years from 2008 and 2009. It consisted of interviewing 26 leaders of Protestant churches and 3 leaders from Catholic churches and the collecting of answers from 123 of 200 people who were believers and pastors in the Protestant Church of a survey of 50 questions. The topic of my research was 'the reason for the explosion of Korean Christian believers'.

While I was doing this research, I also did research in the libraries of Fuller Theological Seminary and Union Theological Seminary in America. As I mentioned earlier, due to that cruel history there were not many related printed materials in Korea and many Korean Christians went to America to study, so many such materials were available in America.

At first, when I started to gather the data on Korean Christian population, I thought if I went to Korea there would at least be a year book, an almanac or chronology and I looked around Seoul City for the data. However, after all I could not find such records on the annual data although there were fragments. I think there never was that kind of data to be found anywhere. As an example of this, the only data for 1941 during the colonization period by Japan which was published by the Korean Governor General within the Christianity Almanac of Japan and was listed in an index of religions and ceremonies in Korea. I found this in the National Diet Library in Tokyo after I returned to Japan. It was special data which could only be viewed in a special room and copying or even taking photos was prohibited.

This data is very important and the last recorded data until the end World War II. According to that data, the total Christian population on the Korean peninsula was a little more than 500,000 of which Catholic Christians consisted of about 120,000 and Protestants made up the remaining 380,000. (At that time, Japanese Christians numbered about 340,000).

If a Korean researcher wants to research as I did, they would not be able to do so without visiting the National Diet Library in Japan. I felt ashamed after I found out why this was the situation. At first I thought I would simply just begin to gather information by checking in to publishers and information repositories in all of Seoul City, but I discovered that in Korea they had endured such a severe oppression where they were unable to even keep records for 36 years spanning the Japanese colonization period.

The reason for the Korean Christian Explosion

In the process of my study I researched about what was behind the sudden large growth of Christianity in Korea and made a questionnaire consisting of 50 questions. The result of that survey administered to pastors and believers suggests that the reason could be as follows:

- There was fervent prayer by Christians
- In honor to the martyrs of the past
- Continued to positively influence medical and social welfare and education
- Pastors worked hard
- Believers diligently studied the Bible
- Believers faithfully worked for missions
- The Nevius Style of mission worked very well
- The pureness of Korean ethnicity allowed for easy acceptance of Christian ideals
- Churches taught proper values to the people while the economy grew

On the other hand, when I first began this research, I thought the following would be the reasons, but that was not exactly the case.

- Cities were expanding quickly
- The fear of Communist attack caused people to turn to the church
- Korean nationalism and Christianity go well together

I discovered through the results of the survey the reason is that Korean people think that peoples' minds played a more important role than outside forces such as political or environmental reasons.

Three times I visited churches in Korea before I started this research, and I visited there 3 more times to conduct interviews and administer this questionnaire. I visited churches and church groups main offices, university and research centers, sometimes pastors' homes, and talked with individuals. One of the big impressions I received was wherever I went people were always saying "I'm praying for Japan" when I took leave of them. I will talk more about this later.

After that, I examined the results of the 50 items on my questionnaire applying a research method called the KJ Method (Kawakita Jiro Method). I'm not talking about the process as contents, but the results were the following three reasons:

1. The Christian religion charmed the Korean people
2. The pureness of the Korean ethnic character went well with Christianity
3. The history of martyrdom gave people trust in Christianity

That is to say, I concluded through my research that these 3 reasons were the main forces behind Korea suddenly becoming a Christian country following World War II.(13)

Korean "Han (한 恨)"

As soon as I started my research I became interested in a dissertation that stated Korean Christianity was greatly influenced by common religions including Confucianism. It was a doctoral dissertation titled "The Growth of the Korean Protestant Church" which was submitted to a university in Holland by J.T. Kim. J.T. Kim was a protestant pastor who lived in America. In that dissertation, Mr. Kim proposed the thesis that the Korean Christian church was greatly influenced by Korean common religions such as Shamanism and Animism. This was a very intriguing thesis.

Even before I started my research, I also had the image that Korean churches were influenced a lot by Confucianism and Shamanism. However, with the progress of my research, I came to think there were deeper roots besides the influence of Confucianism or other religions. Before Confucianism entered Korea, people who lived on the small peninsula placed at the North East edge of Asia must have been raised with one distinct ethnicity under the four clearly separated seasons. This is the ethnicity which I refer to as "pureness".

Regarding Korean ethnic character, Mr. Choe GilSeong (최길성 崔吉城) gives an interesting opinion in his book "Anthropology of Han". He explains Korean ethnic character in relation to the Chinese character "Han". Korean people who were oppressed under the feudalistic system for more than 500 years, then for the time controlled by Japanese guns, had surrendered to a feeling of eternal hopelessness and sadness, and the expression of this feeling is the definition of this Chinese character "Han".(14)

"Han" is explained in a standard Korean dictionary as such a grudge and resentment or sadness which causes a feeling of great antagonism and a desperate hope for relief. It never means just to hold a grudge or be hateful. For example, you can hear this common kind of expression: There is no more Han with my children having grown up well and my having lived a long life of 80 years.

However I was feeling that these people of the Korean peninsula had an ethnic character which came from the old ages and their geologically and climatically affected environments and not from having been under a feudalistic system of government for over 500 years. In other words, my assumption was Korean people have this regional pureness before the introduction of Confucianism. You can say this pureness bloomed from the Zhu Xi school of neo-Confucianism and theological conservatism of Christianity. I will cover this point a little more later.

The connection of pureness and Christian belief

The pureness of Koreans ethnic character is not only an opinion held by me. Pastor Kim IckWon, a Korean Methodist, mentions in his doctoral dissertation titled *A study of the Korean Church growth in context of Korean national characteristics* the seeking of pureness as part of Korean ethnic character and that having been a major driving force in the growth of Christianity in Korea. (15) There is a fair amount of research when speaking of the relationship of ethnic character and Christian ideals referring to the following: "a search for eternity", "creativity", "a mentality of sacrifice", and "being free and uninhibited". However, I think pureness lies at the base of the foundation of all of these arguments or opinions.

You can say the pureness I mentioned is the pureness of a child. This character is to fully trust once the decision to trust has been made, to whole-heartedly try when you decide to do something, to cry loudly if you fail to reach the goal, and then return back to yourself soon and no longer consider the failure. Also in this way to fully laugh when receiving praise, to shed tears when scolded, and loudly protest when someone betrays you.

I am not sure how Koreans might feel about my opinion of their character. I am not an anthropologist or sociologist, so I cannot go into this topic any more deeply. However, in my view the ethnic character of the Korean Church is one of pureness.

Some people say that Korean character is to rush with always saying *"Bballi! Bballi!"* (빨리 빨리 Hurry! Hurry!) And others say Koreans have *"HwaByung"* (화병 火病 "anger illness"). "HwaByung" is defined in the Korean dictionary as a sickness where "you cannot solve a grudging feeling and a problem has developed on your liver" and "you have a headache and pain in the side of your lower abdomen", and "having a congested feeling in your heart and the inability to sleep". Women in their 30s to 50s suffer from this illness the most. If you talk about this critically you would say their ethnicity is too emotional, but I feel this comes from pureness or honesty.

The pureness I see would be expressed as follows:

1. The pureness of human character stems from inception when God first created man and it is a positive character.
2. The pureness of human character shown in Korean ethnic character stems from the geological influence of living on the edge of North East Asia as a small peninsula.
3. The pureness of Korean character may have bloomed from Confucianism but originally was rooted in the innate character of those living on the peninsula.

Korea is sometimes referred to as the "Hermit Kingdom" or "The country of bright morning", but in the same manner as Japan, it has many gangsters, criminals, and suicides. If you look at the negative aspects, there would be many. Yet from the beginning this race has had a deep character, and that would be the pureness.

The race with this characteristic of pureness is drawn to God's son Jesus Christ who was sacrificed on the cross. The God of the Bible is a God who has pureness of character. This means Christianity which is a very simple and pure religion and a race who has the pureness of a child came together. Then, under the difficulties experienced by the country, Christians shed the blood of martyrdom which was the seed of the explosion in the growth of Christianity in Korea, and this is the conclusion I drew from my research

In the next chapter let us explore the manner in which the numbers of Christians increased and the changes in society.

Chapter 3 – The Road to Becoming a Christian Country

Section 1 Prayerful People

Christian believers increased at historical rates

It was not easy to understand, but people started to go to church. This movement began in the 1970s.

Spreading the gospel of Christianity has been going on all over the world since the age of Jesus Christ's first disciples until now, but the number of believers in Korea after World War II suddenly increased with a hard curved line after a rate of low increase that spanned 160 years as seen in the graphs on pages 95-96. This is an example of historic growth.

As I wrote before: 1. A religion with pure teachings, 2.to a race who has a mind filled with pureness, 3. under a history of severe oppression and martyrdom came together and was trusted, so it was quickly and widely accepted. You will see these three reasons are related and gave birth to this result while reading the stories and explanations I am writing in this book.

The explosion in numbers of Christians in Korea did not spring from one single isolated reason. For example, there have been many martyrs in history and surely had a great influence on the minds of Koreans, but even that fact could not be the sole cause of the success of missionaries with similar histories all over the world not resulting in the same kind of explosion in the numbers of Christians in other countries.

When you ask of Korean Christians "what made Korea become a Christian country?", you will be surprised by the number of people answering that the reason is there are many prayerful minded people in

Korea. In fact this was the top result in response to my questionnaire. What made praying be a thing of such great power? You can say it is because it is one of the most religious aspects or it is an aspect of human nature.

According to the Bible everything in the universe is moving by God's will, so if you want to spread the gospel to people, before going to spread the word on your own will you have to ask to God. This is because even though you worked hard there would not be acceptance of God by others unless it was God's will. So the core of the success of missionaries comes first from praying for God's merciful mind to save that person and then to guide them. If this prayer was acceptable to God, the Holy Spirit would work in these people and they would become believers as is taught in the Bible. Korean Christians believed these words and prayed hard. This means Korean Christians with a child's pure belief believed in the power of the Almighty God which is the start of the growth of Christianity.

During the research interviews, I asked to 29 church leaders and researchers about the origins of the Korean Christians' fervent praying which exhibited itself in the Morning Prayer meetings and the Friday Evening prayer meetings which I want to discuss. Half of those people surprised me because they answered with a question of their own about why I was asking that kind of question. It means they thought one should of course be praying if one believed in God.

As to the other half of 14 people, 7 people answered that fervent prayer is an action only stemming from belief, and the other 7 answered that it might have come from their ethnic character. In conclusion, Korean Christians are thinking their attendance of morning and evening prayer meetings is a matter of course for any Christian. I am almost certain to them that for me asking this kind of question appeared as though I did not have enough belief of my own. This fact also shows the pure mind of Korean people.

Number of Christians in the Korean Peninsula (Data for only South Korea after the 1950s)

Year	Catholic believers	Protestant believers	Total population	% Christians
		---	---	
1784	First missions	---	---	
	4,000(1788)	---	---	
	---	---	---	
	9,000(1831)	---	---	
1884	20,000	First missions	---	
1890	17,000	165	---	
1900		20,000	---	
1910	38,000	160,000	13,000,000	1.5
1920	89,000	190,000	16,000,000	1.7
1930	58,000	240,000	19,000,000	1.6
1940	111,000	380,000	22,000,000	2.2
(Below this South Korea data only)				
1950	156,000	600,000	20,000,000	3.8
1960	430,000	1,500,000	25,000,000	7.7
1970	788,000	3,193,000	31,500,000	12.6
1980	1,400,000	7,180,000	38,000,000	22.6
1990	2,400,000	11,880,000	40,000,000	35.7
2000	4,071,560	12,000,000	46,400,000	34.6
2010	5,200,000	12,100,000	48,500,000	35.7

Number of Christians in the Korean Peninsula (Data for only South Korea after the 1950s)

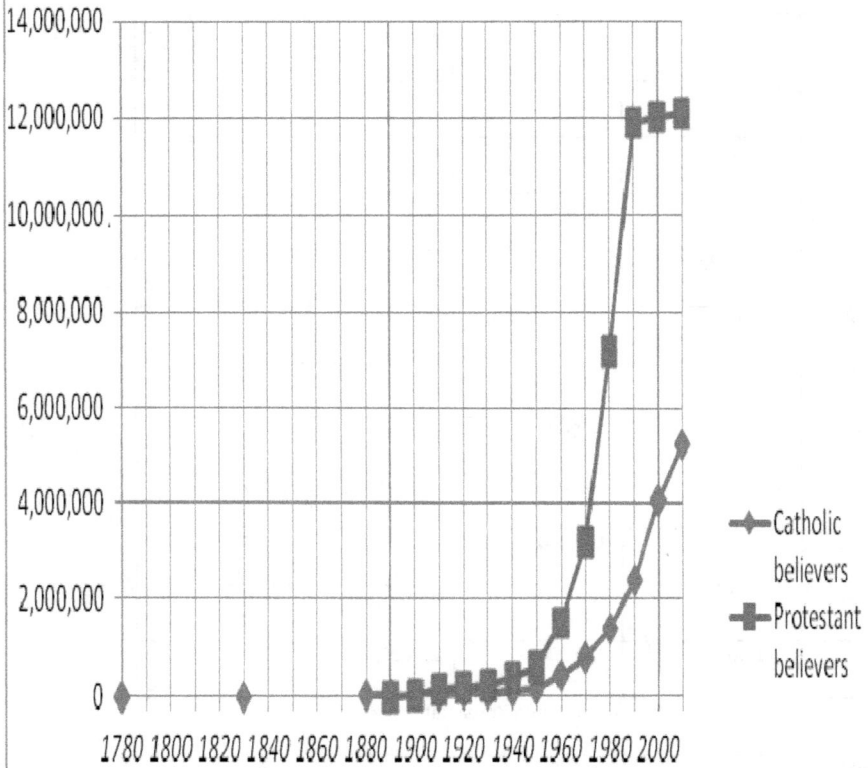

Morning Prayer Meeting

The average temperature in January in Seoul is -3.4 Degrees Celcius, and it is the dead of winter. In that weather at around 4:00AM there are the shadows of many citizens walking along the frozen streets. Every one of them was sucked into the church building. Nowadays there are many people travelling there by car and church parking lots are full. A lot of church members are attending the Morning Prayer Meetings. This is not a recent event but something that began one hundred years ago from the tradition of Korean churches.

The origin of this tradition of Morning Prayer Meeting at Korean churches can be seen very clearly. There was a pastor named Gil SeonJu (길선주 吉善宙) in PyeongYang. He was a very spiritual person and a moving speaker. In 1906 on the Korean peninsula Japanese attacked and the pressure was rising around the time of the Russo-Japanese War. He started holding Morning Prayer Meeting at his church, ChangDaeHyeon Presbyterian Church. In other words, under the national crisis which was caused by the attack of the Japanese, this prayer meeting began for trying to save the country. This was the origin of Morning Prayer Meetings in Korean churches.

Pastor Gil was born in 1869 and married when he was 12 years old according to custom at the time. He was very skilled at "Han Si", writing poetry in Chinese characters. He was at first a follower of Buddhism but later was converted to Christianity and was baptized at age 29. When he was 34, he entered PyeongYang Seminary and studied the Bible, and in 1906 when he was 37 years old he began this Morning Prayer meeting at ChangDaeHyeon Presbyterian Church.

Not only Pastor Gil SeonJu was praying there, but also the missionaries who had guided him were there praying fervently. In the end, every Korean pastor has this trait of earnest prayerfulness. Step by step, everything in the Korean churches came to be started, continued and finished with prayer. Believers were also educated in an environment of prayer. The revival in PyeonYang in 1907 which I mentioned before also occurred from this environment. I feel sorry because I cannot express precisely in my writing about Koreans' feelings that everything depends on prayer.

I will introduce an event which occurred during that time. On Saturday, January 14th in 1907 pastors from the Methodist and Presbyterian churches opened a revival meeting together at PyeonYang-ChungAng Church. There were around 1,500 people gathered, and those who could not get into the building were worshipping while standing outside. A missionary William N. Blair gave the following sermon:

If there is a brother in pain, all Christians have to share that pain. If a church member feels jealousy, that would not only be hurting all other church members' minds but also felt by Jesus Christ who is the head of the church. That can be exactly compared to feeling pain all over your body if you hurt only your little finger.(16)

People heard this sermon and felt the pain in their mind and began to earnestly repent and crying loudly. In other words, group repentance occurred. Those people who had this experience shared their feelings about this event with their family and friends, and those who heard this story started to attend church.

This is only one example story. In Korea, there are many of these stories.

In 1890, 6 years after the start of Protestant missions, church believers still only numbered 165, but 20 years later in 1910 the numbers had grown to 160,000 which I mentioned before. I also wrote before about the 3 main reasons for the great increase of Christians in Korea, but when you think about this kind of story, I think that the first reason must be that Christianity itself has its own large, attractive charm.

Since that time one hundred years have passed, but Korean churches continue to have Morning Prayer meetings to this day. An example of this can be seen here that in 1995 at the MyeongSeong Presbyterian Church which has 30,000 members and every morning a total of 16,000 believers are attending Morning Prayer meetings that are held at 4:30, 5:30, 6:30 and 10:00AM.

In July of 2010, I attended as a guest a National Breakfast Prayer Meeting which was held at the Coex Convention and Exhibition Center in Seoul City. This Breakfast Prayer Meeting began at 6:30 and is commonly called Presidential Breakfast Prayer Meeting with President Lee MyeongBak (이명박 李明博)attending. I was surprised to see that 3000 regular citizens attended that meeting. After a sermon and a prayer from a church representative, breakfast was served for the entire crowd of 3000, and the crowd dispersed quickly after the meal.

Morning Prayer Meeting is now spread around the world as the image of Korean Christian church. A long time ago Catholic monks were charged with the duty of praying 7 times a day. One of those praying times was in the middle of the night and they had to awake and pray and then return to sleep. Another praying time was 5:00 AM. Even in Japan nowadays too, Buddhist monks also practice asceticism. Religion having early morning activities is not an unusual thing. However, in Korea, there are so many people participating in Morning Prayer Meetings. Even regular church goers are attending church once a week or every day attending Morning Prayer Meetings.

This service is not continuing to pray for an entire hour. First a hymn is sung, then one of the representatives or the pastor prays, scripture from the Bible is read, a sermon is delivered, the pastor prays, and after that people pray aloud their individual prayers together as a group. That prayer rises throughout the building and sounds as though it is reaching as far as heaven. At the last, after the pastor's blessing, people return home or go on their way to their workplace. Prayer Meeting in Korean churches means not only meeting for prayer but is the same style as a

Sunday morning worship service.

Evening Prayer Meeting – Fasting Prayer – Prayer on the Mountain

Among the Korean Protestant churches there are churches which hold
evening services every Friday night from 7:00. Even though it is called
CheolYa Prayer Service (철야기도회 : "all through the night"), it is not
usually lasting all night and consists of Bible reading, praying, and
private meditation time. It is just a small service like the Morning Prayer
meetings and usually finishes after about one hour. After that, some
people return to their homes, while others may continue until 10:00PM
or stay and attend another prayer meeting which begins at 11:00PM.
There are some people who then return home after that 11:00 meeting
finishes, but there are others who without sleeping continue to pray
and read scriptures until the Morning Prayer service at 5:00AM. This is a
true example of a CheolYa Service.

There are also a fair amount of Christians who fast at least once a week.
They do not eat any food, and only drink water while reading the Bible
or praying. There are some people who fast for one or two days during
their days off from work. Some people would be surprised to hear of
people fasting for 2 or 3 days, but it does not appear to be anything out
of the ordinary to those who are doing this. There are a fairly large
number of wealthier Protestant churches in Korea who maintain a
facility for fasting and prayer separate from their church building. Those
places have a pastor who always stays there, and several workers are
taking care of the facilities. In the corner of the large floor there are
stacks of blankets for taking a short nap. There is also a small restaurant
for making rice soup for eating after fasting has finished.

Most of the facilities for fasting and prayer are built outside of the city
or in the mountains. In Japan there are some religions that practice

asceticism in the mountains, and this is also true in Korea. There has long been this kind of tradition of fasting and praying in the mountain. It could happen that one might find a new way to live while being in the calm mountains while reading the Bible and meditating individually. People who feel exhausted in their relationships, people who failed in private business, or people about to begin their own business are going into the mountain to pray. There are several of these kinds of facilities which can hold as many as 10,000 people. This kind of facility does not need to serve food, so they only need to have water, toilets, and floor space for people to take a short nap. The people there spend their day with their water bottle, prayer, reading the Bible, and sometimes attending small services which are held regularly throughout the day. There are also special cases of people as a last resort going there when they have been diagnosed with fatal illnesses where the doctors have said there was no hope of recovery. There are real examples of people being cured there and living with their deep belief for the rest of their lives.

There are some work places which have their own areas for prayer meetings. In 2008 in the hotel where I had been staying, at 6:00AM people, either by themselves or in pairs, came by car with their Bibles to a prayer meeting there. I heard before that once a month in the early morning businessmen in that city held a prayer meeting in the hotel banquet hall or restaurant, and it must have been one of those kinds of prayer meetings. Some factory workers hold this kind of meeting as well during lunch time, every day, or one or two times a week. In the military also some soldiers are gathering for this kind of meeting, and there are officers-only meetings, too.

Why are they cherishing this kind of prayer meeting this much? It is because the attraction of praying to Christians is that believers can think about God who is beside them, draw closer to God (the Father and Jesus Christ), receive the Holy Spirit, and find joy in meeting God in their mind's eye. In Christianity this is called "spiritual joy". This means the joy of being spiritually connected to God who created the universe. For them praying means great joy in their mind and that joy would be the power with which they could live out their day.

In a prayer meeting, a sermon can also be heard. They would be encouraged with the feeling that God had directly spoken to them when they have problems or are dealing with other difficulties in their lives. Surprise would be changed to deep emotion when you read a scripture from the Bible where those contents come together with the problems you are having. If you have deep knowledge of the Bible, you will feel the teachings of the Bible will be more closely connected to you. This is one of the attractions of prayer meetings. One of the key factors for the explosion in the number of Korean Christians after World War II came from the power which originated from believers having such internal passionate belief.

Flourishing Bible studies

There is a story that goes like this in the Bible: Jesus Christ said of a woman named Maria who was calmly listening to His stories that her actions were more correct than the woman named Martha who was working busily to serve the people. We who are human often think that performing a service activity for welfare or being a volunteer is a more religious act than studying the Bible or praying. About this Jesus Christ said that working hard or performing these acts is important, but above those it is more important to listen to God's voice. In this way, you can say that Christianity is a religion of study. The Bible tells us who is the creator of this universe, who are people, what is the true meaning of status, honor, and wealth, what a human's life is, and then about marriage, home, and families.

These early missionaries earnestly taught the Bible. People also studied the Bible with joy. The first work of early missionaries who applied the Nevius Style which I mentioned before was teaching the Bible. Korean pastors who were taught by those missionaries also earnestly taught the Bible to believers in their churches with their sermons on Sunday or sometimes opened Bible study meetings almost every day. The Bible is a large textbook but not difficult. Through sermons and services every Sunday or the lectures of meetings, believers learned step by step about the Bible for all of their lives. In Korea Bible study is greatly flourishing.

Normally churches are led by a head pastor. This is because even though there are several associate pastors, the shepherd of a church can be only one as there is only one God. However always listening to only the sermons of one pastor it is easy to fall into a rut. That is why once or twice a year in Korean Protestant Churches special lecturers are invited to speak or special meetings are held which last from 2 to 5 days in a row.

Special lecturers give sermons about 4 times; in the early morning, mid-morning, afternoon, and at night. This will continue like this for several days. A good speaker will be invited as a guest lecturer. The speaker will allow the listeners to laugh, cry, and be moved, but is also not forgetting to admonish them. This is an interesting story time not like a strict lecture in school.

Conservative interpretation of the Bible

For interpreting the Bible there are differences based on how a pastor grew up or the education they received. Of course this would also influence the believers of their churches. From the last of the 18th Century to the first of the 19th Century the background, character, specialties and other aspects of the 66 books of the Bible were extensively researched. The Bible was studied from a scientific and critical view.

Being based on the results of this research made the sermons of pastors similar to lectures in university. Basically speaking these kinds of sermons were difficult sermons. In Japan the criticism is often made that sermons are delivered in this style. However, in Korea pastors are often giving sermons after understanding the Bible scriptures well and focusing on the useful aspects that relate to daily life in their sermons.

If you consider either scientific or critical interpretation of scriptures of the Bible as being progressive, then the interpretation of the Bible by Korean pastors would be deemed conservative. If you interpret Bible scriptures as either scientific or critical you cannot deny that the overall view of the authority of the scriptures as being Holy would be lessened, but in Korea Christians interpret the scriptures conservatively so they hold the scriptures of the Bible as most holy and spread the Word as the authority. (The theology of the Korean Protestant Church is illustrated in the books "The History of Theological Ideas in Korean Christianity" and "Korean Christianity" translated into Japanese by Yoo DongSik (유동식 柳東植).)

Pastor Choong BoonGwan in his master's thesis submitted at the Fuller Theological Seminary in America "Thoughts of Social Structures in Korea and the Growth of the Church" says the conservatism of the Korean church stems from the family system of patriarchy found in Confucianism. In other words, the loyalty to a king or parents found in Confucianism influences the loyalty to Christ and permeates the conservative atmosphere of the Korean church.

Some people insist the character of Koreans has innate emotional aspects, and others are saying that the working of Koreans' brains are divided into 70% right-brain and 30% left with the right brain as the emotional side while the left is the logical side. Japanese people are said to be the opposite with 30% right-brain and 70% left-brain. This means that Japanese people are seen as being better suited for things that lend themselves toward more logical thinking and making elaborate machinery while Koreans tend to be more creative. I think Korean

Christians' ability to hear and be moved by sermons is related to this, and the sermons of pastors are in response to this.

Section 2 "Red Cross"

The miracle of HanGang (한강 漢江)

After the Korean War and after passing through many difficulties in the previous years, the economic policies of the Korean government saw some success, and in the 1970s the Korean economy grew and entered a time of prosperity. This was similar to the high growth of Japan in the 1960s. This means that the time of prosperity came 10 years later than the one in Japan. This is because while Japan was beginning recovery from World War II in 1945, Korea was still involved in the Korean War for 8 more years until 1953. In the 1970s the GNP was 254 dollars, but in the 1980s the GNP experienced a sudden growth by a multiple of 6 to 1,645 dollars. Products for export had been clothing and daily living items but changed to heavy chemical and industrial products. People around the world called this economic prosperity in Korea of the 1970s "the miracle of HanGang". "HanGang" is the name of the river flowing through the middle of Seoul City. The big city of Seoul experienced sudden growth.

In Japan there is a "Dankaino Sedai" (団塊の世代 : Baby-boom Generation) after World War II. In Korea also, 8 years later than the start of the one in Japan a Baby-boom Generation started. In Korea the same as Japan that term did not last for very long and the numbers of young people in the population began to decrease. However when this Baby-boom Generation was a productive part of society from ages 18 to 59 the numbers of Christians increased greatly.

The population began to migrate from the countryside to the big city, especially the cities of Seoul and Busan. The change of the population in Seoul City rapidly increased as is noted in the following:

1945   850,000

1961   2,690,000

1980   8,500,000

2008   10,320,000

In 1930, in Pre-World War II Korea, the total population of citizens who lived in cities was less than 5%, but by the late 1970s the number had risen to 60%. To say that in the mid 1960s the agrarian population was higher than 60% sounds like a lie. Within about 10 years there was a reversal in the percentage of the population of countryside dwellers and city dwellers. The urbanization was that rapid.

Seoul City was developed on the north side of the river HanGang. Because of the increase in the city population, from the late 1970s, the city began to develop to the south of the river. In the 1970s there were still apartment buildings that were only 4 or 5 floors tall, but by the year 2000, groups of tens to hundreds of buildings in apartment complexes of 15, even 20 floors high had appeared. Foreign businessmen who visited Korea for business must have been surprised by the changes to Seoul City every single time they visited. Nowadays, there are about 20 bridges spanning the HanGang River, and Seoul City does not feel like it is divided by the HanGang.

This abrupt change destroyed the social foundation Korea had before which was concentrated in the countryside. The uniqueness of Korean society which is based on MoonJung (a relative grouping based on living in the area of the cemeteries holding their ancestors' tombs) still continues but various aspects had no other choice but to change. The relatives who have moved to the cities began new relationships and created groups called JongChin-Hwe (종친회 宗親会 : which is like a sort of branch of MoonJung). This is a special case, but I heard that some JongChin-Hwe gather as many as 20,000 people. Furthermore, it is prohibited by law for JongChin-Hwe to show any support of specific candidates in national elections. In Japan, there would commonly be brothers helping brothers economically, but not to other lesser relatives. Yet in Korea a group like JongChin-Hwe is even giving economic support to its members. In the middle of the rapid society change, the system of the old society still continued.

As in Japan in 1958 a singer named Frank Nagai had a hit song titled "Yuraku-chode Aimasyo" (有楽町で会いましょう : Let's meet at a place named Yuraku-cho), in 1972 in Korea a singer named Nam Jin had a hit song titled "Nimgwa hamgge" (님과 함께 : Together With My Darling). The lyrics of the song contain the words "On that green grassy range, I want to build a house like a picture, and with my love, my darling live together for a hundred years..." Both songs have a feeling of the finish of the old ages and a new age beginning.

Peoples' lives also began to change. Especially the development of nation-wide thoroughfares changed things because if someone departed Seoul in the early morning they could reach any place in Korea within the same day, and the distance could be travelled within 5 hours. Roofs made from woven rice stalks were changed to slate and then soon to concrete buildings. Even a small village on an island had electricity and television. Before they drank only water, but now they drink tea. Even though it is slightly different, Korean people experienced nearly everything we Japanese experienced after World War II. The thing that changed the most was that every village was filled with many children. The people of that Baby-boom Generation grew up, and in 1974 the percentage of male students who continued on to attain a middle school education was higher than 50%. Required education was still only through elementary school. However the percentage of female students who continued on to middle school remained very low.

The Sae-Maeul Movement (새마을 운동 : The New Village Movement)

In the 1970s at the same time as the Miracle of HanGang of economic development another big change was taking place in Korean society. It was the Sae-Maeul Movement. In the phrase Sae-Maeul, "Sae" means "new" and "Maeul" means "village". This was the movement of modernization of the villages in the countryside. Until that time, people were still using foot-powered rice thrashing machines, but after that people began to use engine-powered thrashing machines. Pesticides were widely used and crop production greatly increased.

Non-Christian Korean families have the tradition "Wi-Pae" (위패 位牌 : memorial tablets for the names of deceased family members and ancestors) according to Confucianism, which is similar to "Butsudan (仏壇)" in Japan, and kept it well. Furthermore in the same manner as that of Japan, the tombs of family members are also well kept. On New Year's Day, the Day of Passing Memorial, and certain days of Confucianism all relatives (MoonJung) gather together in front of that tomb and perform a special ceremony. However, because Korean society abruptly changed from a fixed agrarian society to a modern citizenry gathering all relatives together as before became difficult, and Korean tombs which were covered with mounds of dirt took up too much space (*the average area was 7-8 "tsubo" in Japanese or "pyeong" in Korean – about 250 to 285 sq ft – and all together covering about 1% of the land in Korea*) causing the government to enact laws limiting their size and recommend cremation instead (*In 2000, the national percentage of those choosing cremation was about 30% while in Seoul City it was as much as 83%*).

At the same time, the folk belief called "Goot (굿)" also was affected. "Goot" means a shamanistic ritual with song and dance and spiritual possession where a shaman utters an incantation allowing a spirit to enter her body and then speak through her and this ritual was very common in Korea. Because this kind of ritual was considered as a superstitious belief or black magic, people spoke out against continuing this ritual. This was also an aspect of the Sae-Maeul Movement.

A young man when he was 16 years old had a spirit come upon him, and he began to tell the future and the spirit talked through him. This kind of behavior was called "Goot", and a picture or symbol was placed on a shelf that was called "Goot-Dan" similarly to "Butsudan" in Japan. Later he worked at several different occupations, finished his military duty, and married. After that, he restarted his spiritual work. However, because his children grew up disliking their father's work, in 1975 when he turned 45 years old, he converted to Buddhism and tore down his "Goot-Dan", built a temple, and became a monk.

Like this person in Korea, Confucianism, Folk Belief, Animism, or Buddhism are overlapping instead of standing against each other as different religions. Part of the Sae-Maeul Movement was to remove this old-fashioned view of religion.(17) The removal of the custom of creating "JokBo" (족보 族譜 : family tree) and displaying their family positions which I mentioned before also was a part of the Sae-Maeul Movement.

However, later, with the progress of urbanization and the collapse of the agrarian society the Sae-Maeul Movement burned out in the late 1990s.

The Third Change: the explosion of Protestant believers

On the other hand, in the 1970s there was another big change, the Third Change, which appeared. That was the explosion of the numbers of Christian believers. The number of Protestant believers in 1970 was 3,190,000, but by the 1980s that number had increased to 7,180,000 which means that within 10 years the numbers had increased by almost

4,000,000. The number of Catholic believers went from 780,000 to 1,400,000 during the same time period. This increase is not normal and is very rare in the history of the Christian church in the world. Throngs of people poured into the church. This was more than 22% of the entire population of 38,120,000. New Churches were built every week. Especially the increase in the numbers of Protestant believers was monumental. At this time visitors from Japan travelling to Korea must have been surprised to see church spirals or red crosses in windows everywhere. All of those were representing Protestant churches. The red color of the crosses symbolized the blood of Jesus Christ. To Japanese, the color red means to be cautious, so a red cross would not be seen as a positive symbol. Yet to Koreans the cross image could not exist without the color red. Here also I see a difference of ethnicity.

If you count the number of Christian believers in Japan, this includes Protestant and Catholic believers together, but in Korea Protestant believers are called "GyeShin-Gyo (개신교 改新教)" and Catholics are called "CheonJoo-Gyo (천주교 天主教)" and regarded as a separate religion.

In 2008 just before I began my research, I heard the number of Christian believers in Korea was between 20 and 25% of the population, and I thought of this number as including both Catholics and Protestants although actually this number only reflects the number of Protestant believers.

The Debut of Korean churches in the world

In 1973 I was in Atlanta in America conducting in the field surveys researching about revival events which were held by the missionary group named the Billy Graham Evangelistic Association. In the Christian church in America there is a history of holding mega-events for revivals which gathered people in the tens of thousands.

One day in the summer I was in the office of an official of that association when he announced the historical results achieved at an event held by Billy Graham in Korea which had gathered more than 1,000,000 people and everyone in the office cheered and applauded. At the time I heard this news I did not know exactly what that meant, but the word spread all around the world and surprised many people. It meant that was the day Korea debuted as a Christian country to the world. In Japan, Pastor Billy Graham is not very well known, but among Protestant Christian believers around the world, he is the most highly regarded pastor. Because this person had gathered more than 1,000,000 people to a single event this garnered attention around the world.

The number of one million is not an exaggeration. At that time I was researching about revival events in the American church that gathered people in the tens of thousands, and the attendance numbers are taken very accurately to avoid criticism about being exaggerated or appearing misleading. In America and Korea the leader of the association began meticulously preparing one year ahead for this event. Large video monitors and speakers were placed all around so that everyone in attendance could hear the speech clearly. The place the event was held was a place like Tiananmen Square in China which is on the reclaimed land of Yeoui-do Square and is now called Yeoui-do Park located in front of the National Assembly Building.

From about this time all around the world you could hear things being said such as "in Korea Christians believers are exploding" and "in Korea miracles are happening", "in Korea almost 1/3 of the nationally elected officials are Christians". That revival event led by Pastor Billy Graham which gathered 1,000,000 people was when Korea debuted on the world stage as being recognized as being Christian and one of the big turning points of the Korean Christian Church. It was a symbolic event as the bright light signaled the future to the "white-clothed people" who had experienced a history of great hardships and to the country which had the image of the sad Arirang Song.

An example of a local church

The growth of the Korean church mainly happened in urban areas, but you cannot say the countryside did not grow as well. I will give an example of a church in the 1970s in an area with a population of about 100,000. It is a Presbyterian Church which I will call "Church A" which is placed inland slightly east of the middle of the peninsula.

This Church A was founded in 1924 and was concerned about having not grown while under the persecution of the Japanese Army. After the Korean War the numbers increased naturally, and in 1972 it became a mid-sized church in the local community with attendance of 293 believers. Ten years later in 1982 the numbers had increased to 390. Even with this growth when compared to the national average this was a low percentage, but the attendance of each Sunday worship service ranged from 358 to 584. 259 people were baptized during this ten year period. Even though some Christians moved into the area and church, 386 believers moved away to the larger cities of Seoul or Busan. When you consider this point, this church was doing very well over all.

In 1922, including Church A there were 28 churches in that area with a total of 11,000 people attending. This means that was about 11% of the population which is not as much as the national average of 19%, but for that area it reflected a big change. High schools, orphanages, facilities for women, facilities for the elderly, Bible schools, and hospitals were among the kinds of facilities opened and maintained by Christians and contributed to the betterment of the lives of citizens. Yet the most significant contribution among those was that before there was only the age-old feudalistic atmosphere, but now it was a changed mentality to a bright atmosphere of caring about others.

In the 1970s church members when viewed by occupation saw that about half were middle class citizens of trained professionals, company office workers, government officials, and small business owners, and the other half were farmers, factory workers and others in the lower income class. The number of college graduates was estimated at 23%, high school graduates was 42%, middle school graduates were 13%, and elementary school graduates were 18.5%. 86% of the attendees could travel on foot to church within 20 minutes. Only 5% took more than 40 minutes travel time to reach the church. The age of attendees regularly covers all ages.

On Sunday three chapel services were held: one in the morning at 10:00, 11:30, and again in the evening at 7:30 with all of them lasting about one hour each. Every morning from 4:30 to 6:00 Morning Prayer Meeting was held. Every Wednesday evening from 7:30 to 9:00 a Prayer Meeting was held, and every Friday evening a Bible meeting was held at someone's residence. The activities are similar to other churches, and this is one of the ordinary local churches.

Sunday chapel means that there was Sunday school (Bible study meetings held for about an hour with classes separated by age groups), Sunday school has classes ranging from age 4, elementary school students, middle school students, high school students, youths, adults (older than 32 years old), and usually consists of 9 different classes. The pastor or teachers are leading this school. One of the groups is for the hearing impaired. Furthermore church attendees are divided by their residential areas into 30 groups which hold Bible study meetings regularly.

This kind of local church opened one by one during the 1970s.

The percentage of church growth

In Korea there were several criteria for measuring church growth. Not every Korean church agrees, but growth is measured for example by the number of people attending, size of the financial budget, mission goals, retaining current level of percentage of population in attendance whether the population goes up or down, or reaching goals of a higher percentage of numbers of attendees, or even by goals which cannot accurately be measured by numbers and must be considered from other aspects. There are some who hold the opinion that to measure the growth of religious groups is inappropriate, so talking about church growth is a very rare thing, yet this is an aspect of the Korean church during the 1970s.

On the other hand, they are talking about the increase in the numbers of believers. For example over the last 10 years an increase of 25% is seen as low, and an increase of 100% or doubling is seen as good. An increase of 500% is seen as super good. In this way, if you apply this rule to Church A for 10 years from 1972 to 1982 the increase in numbers of attendees was 29% so it ranked as slightly better than 'low' and places them in the category of only slightly increasing. When viewed by people from other countries, these numbers would be seen as marvelous or surprisingly high, but in Korea it would be placed in the lower class. This tells us how differently the explosion of growth in the 1970s in Korea occurred.

Section 3-As a rock is moving (1970s)

The case of Pastor Jo YongGi (조용기/ 趙鏞基)

Let's look more deeply into the aspects of the Korean church of the
1970s. The reason for doing this is because for twenty years, this 10
years of the 1970s and the following decade of the 1980s, was the term
in which historical examples of explosions in the numbers of Protestant
Christians took place.

As I mentioned before, the Korean Protestant Church had their
tendencies which were strongly influenced by the Puritan way and
placed great importance on spiritual experience. From the beginning of
the Bible there are mentions of events in daily life of spiritual
experiences such as physical healing and speaking in tongues.

From the first church in history which placed great weight on spiritual
experiences and growing through the church of the times of the Roman
Empire being the national religion, the Church had to educate vast
numbers of citizens about the Bible. The fact this caused a lot of time to
be spent educating people about the Bible and placed relatively less
emphasis on spiritual experiences is a part of church history. After that
the church still placed a high level of importance on being educated
about the Bible, but the spiritual aspects were not completely
overlooked. The importance of spiritual experience was at times held in
higher regard and at times emphasized less.

At the beginning of the 1900s in America, the revival movement of
spiritual experiences was prominent once again, and after World War II
the missionaries from that time came into Korea. Pastor Jo YongGi was
raised in this kind of environment. He was born in 1936 at a home in the
southern region of Korea during the most difficult period of the time of
the Japanese Colonization. His parents were raised in the normal way of
the times of Confucianism and Buddhism. In 1953 (the end of the Korea

War) when he was 17 years old, he contracted tuberculosis too badly to treat and was only waiting to die. A friend of his younger sister introduced him to the church and he was converted to Christianity. Incredibly, he dramatically recovered from his illness.

By chance he met an American missionary who belonged to a church of the Assembly of God, which emphasized spiritual experience. This church was very conservative in their beliefs and interpreted the Bible word for word. The name Assembly of God means a gathering of God and in Japan the church used the English name. In Korea the church is called Hannanim-ui SeongHwe (하나님의 성회 : God's Holy Assembly).

Because the young Jo YongGi had great skill with languages, he interpreted the words of the missionaries as much as his health would allow. He could speak not only English, but also Japanese since he was born in 1936 during the time of the colonization. He not only did interpretation but learned the Bible directly from the missionaries. That was for three years of his late teens. He read the Bible earnestly and realized that in his case he was not living exactly as the Bible taught so he deeply repented. For 3 days he fasted and fervently prayed. On the final day, the image of Jesus appeared to him.

The incredible experience of seeing the image of Jesus would bring unfaltering faith to some, but to those who heard of these experiences the person was sometimes treated as though they might be mentally ill. Seeing this kind of image is an act of God so this kind of occurrence is a spiritual experience. Recorded in the history of Christianity there is a surprisingly large number of people who have had this kind of experience. The types of spiritual experiences vary greatly. The Reformer Martin Luther and John Calvin also had this kind of incredible spiritual experience, and this is connected to a great work of God. A Japanese pastor Masuzaki Sotohiko (升崎外彦 : 1892-1976), who I knew personally, was the son of a Buddhist monk and set to follow the path of becoming a monk himself, but he was converted to Christianity and when he was about to be killed by his father for opposing him, he saw the image of Jesus Christ. Later he was disowned by his father, but he still became a pastor and did a lot of social work until his death. Later in life his father forgave him for becoming a Christian. In this fashion, spiritualism in the church is not uncommon and not seen as out of the ordinary.

The young Jo YongGi traveled up to Seoul when he was twenty years old and registered to enter SoonBokEum Seminary (순복음신학교 純福音神学校 : present day HanSe University). "SoonBokEum" comes from the interpretation of "full gospel" in English and means "filled with the gospel" and "completed with the gospel". In other words this church is saying to not only believe in God the Father and Christ, God's son, but without also believing in the Holy Spirit which is described in the Bible as the Word of God, your belief is not complete. Even though he was in poor health, he persisted in his deep study until he mastered his belief in the Bible word for word.

He met an older lady in that seminary who had worked as a nurse before and now was studying so she could be a witness for Christ. She helped care for and advise the weak and young Jo YongGi. Later the daughter of this lady would marry him. Lady Choe JaSil (최자실 崔子実), who became his mother-in-law, continued to assist him in his work for God. When he was 22 years old, in 1958 with only the help of her and her family, the young Jo YongGi along with Lady Choe JaSil and her three daughters erected a tent in a very poor area of Seoul City. He used the tent as a church and even began preaching on the street. All of the people were living in poor conditions, and the people in this area were particularly poor. These 5 people had almost no income and often had to get by with only having thin rice soup to eat.

Jo YongGi had two special gifts from God. One was the power of speaking well. His speech was filled with belief, hope, and confidence and he taught that if you believe in Jesus Christ, you would not only be spiritually blessed but you could be economically blessed. In other words, he taught that people should live positively. The other gift was spiritual power. When he prayed, many people were healed. One whose body had been paralyzed for 7 years was healed along with many others and even a shaman was converted to Christianity. These events look like those recorded in Acts of the New Testament.

He had not only the gift of healing. Those people who gathered in the tent church were moved by the Holy Spirit and began speaking in tongues. Speaking in tongues means someone was moved and filled with the Holy Spirit and expressed it through their mouth. This is also a kind of spiritual experience. Some people saw images of the future and spoke about that. These kinds of sudden appearances of the Holy Spirit are called the gift of the Holy Spirit and these people were the topic of conversation for many people at that time.

The world's largest mega-church

3 years later there were 600 people attending chapel services held by Jo YongGi, and the tent was replaced with a new church building. The year that church, SoonBokEum JoongAng Church, was built was when he was 26 years old and he was ordained as a pastor. In 1968 when he was 32 years old that church became a large church with over 8000 attendees, and on Sunday it required 3 separate services to accommodate them and still not everyone could enter the buildings, so mats were placed in the parking lots for those left outside during the services.

The church in the Bible is divided into family units. He learned this way of thinking from the Bible and divided and structured area groups with 10 families each as a unit for helping to nurture the growth of their belief. He educated and guided the leaders of the units. 80% of the unit leaders were women. He emphasized learning the Bible and praying diligently to all of the church members. He asked each member to do individual worship every day that included reading the Bible and praying. It is easy to say, but the act is very difficult. He also awoke early in the morning to read the Bible and pray and sometimes fasting and reading the Bible and praying, and even sometimes did this overnight. He not only taught church members to read the Bible and pray but also to visit their neighbors and witness to them.

In this way, the church led by Pastor Jo YongGi in 1973 bought a wide piece of land beside the National Assembly Hall which was called YeoUiDo, reclaimed land, and built YeoUiDo SoonBokEum Church. The number of attendees had reached 18,000, and in 1979 it grew to 100,000 in 1980 doubled to 200,000, and in the Los Angeles Times newspaper in America it was reported as the world's largest Protestant Church. Then in 1992 the number had grown to 700,000 and was sending missionaries to countries all over the world including Japan. According to data from 2003 they had sent about 600 missionaries.

In 2008 Pastor Jo YongGi retired, but the church continued to grow under its successor. During the year from 2008 to 2009, membership grew by 15,000 people, and each Sunday held services 7 times which continues to this day. While Pastor Jo YongGi was still working, bringing that many people together in one place was problematic, so in order to avoid this issue, he made 19 other churches, and those churches also had 100,000 people in total attending.

It can be said that the appearance of the YeoUiDo SoonBokEum Church was representative as a symbol of the differences of the Protestant Church all over Korea. In every Protestant church the pastor feels that their own church is moving by an invisible power which is like a giant rock which even though it doesn't look like it is moving, it is slowly being moved by an unseen power. Every Sunday more people came to church and their faces brightened at the messages delivered there.

In the 1970s, the explosion of the number of Protestant believers was a great shock to the citizens of Korea. It was a phenomenon and was as though Korea had been appointed some special mission in the world by God. In the not too distant past, there had been tens of thousands of martyrdoms which also had a relationship to the miraculous increase in believers of today.

Prayer of hopeful happiness (기복신앙 祈福信仰)

According to Korean folk religion, in this world there are many gods. Among them the highest is called "Haneul-Nim" (하늘님 : The God of Heaven or the Only God in Heaven). Catholic Christianity which entered Korea in the 18th Century called their own God "Haneu-Nim" (하느님 : "Haneu" means "heaven" and "nim" means "sir") which had the same meaning as the folk religion definition of God. In other words, "God" means the "Only God in Heaven".

However, in the Protestant Church around 1885, the pronunciation was changed only slightly and God was called "Hana-Nim". (하나님 : "Hana" means "the only one" and "nim" means "sir") The reason for the change was to clearly show the difference between the god of the highest level in Korean folk religion and the only God in Christianity even though both groups were using the same meaning of "the only god in heaven".

After all, Shamanism (a religious ceremony where a shaman was the connection between and was interpreting messages from the spirits) was very popular in Korea during the time of the Joseon Dynasty. This was not only in Korea but almost every race and ethnic group in the world has this kind of history. When someone was sick, a shaman acted as the intermediary to pray to the spirits for healing. They made offerings of food to spirits, uttered incantations, and sometimes injured themselves and prayed for the gods to grant them their desires. For any kind of event Korean people visited a shaman (male or female shamans) for consultation and asked for prayers.

Christianity differs fundamentally from shamanism, but if you read the Bible you can see scriptures about Jesus Christ healing many sicknesses at the request of the people. After Christ ascended to heaven, the disciples in the name of Jesus Christ also prayed for healing through the Holy Spirit in answer to requests from the people.

In Japan from the start of the first open missionaries in the Meiji Era, missions focused on teaching the doctrine of the Bible or in making knowledgeable speeches and spreading the Word and didn't follow the route of healing sicknesses. In Korea, without an educational mission approach, missionaries proselytized the practical and immediate benefits through acts such as praying for healing. You can't say every pastor is doing this, but most pastors in Korea are praying for solutions to the current problems of their congregations. This is one of the main reasons for the increase in the number of Christians.

To avoid misunderstanding I will add this; Christians are not teaching that God would supply anything someone requests. If every request man made to God was granted, this world would be unsettled by being overfilled with the greediness of humans. The Korean church is just spreading the word of God that if you believe and depend on the word of God, "Hana-Nim" (the only God in Heaven) will grant all things necessary to you.

This kind of belief of just asking for God's blessing is called "GiBok ShinAng" (Prayer of hopeful happiness), and there are some Christians in Korea who are against this kind of thinking. However, most people are accepting this positively and actively. According to the results of my survey, the first reason for the explosion of the numbers of Christians in Korea is Christianity itself has its own charm, and the first specific reason for this charm was that of loving your neighbor as yourself. The second reason was the teaching that God would bless people in the present.

The "Spurgeon" of Korea

While the number of churches was growing, there were many eloquent pastors who appeared. One of them, Yi SeongBong (이성봉 李聖鳳), in 1950 became the head of SeoMoon Church. SeoMoon Church belonged to the Holiness Union (in Korean called SeonGyeul GyɔDan 성결교단 聖潔教団) group and worked there for 40 years. He is called the "Spurgeon of Korea" because of a comparison of him to a famous orator, Pastor C. H. Spurgeon (1834-1892). Pastor Yi spoke using metaphors about the principles of water.

> Water has no antlers; sharp protruding edges, and even has no fingernails or toenails which are used for scratching someone. Yet water never gives up moving in the direction of its goal. It is always moving forward. When there is something hard in its path, the water divides or moves to either side. If the water is blocked from progressing, it rises up and in the end flows over the thing that was blocking it. Water is always progressing forward towards its goal.(19)

Pastor Yi SoengBong always encouraged his followers that the church also always had to move forward. As in his metaphors, all of the churches in the country progressed on and on. This is the state of the church in the 1970s.

Pastor Yi also recommended to his members that once a year they should donate blood. This is physical manifestation of their belief. In other words he put weight on the idea of believers contributing to society.

In the Korean Protestant Church, there was not only Pastor Yi SeongBong, but there were many other famous orators. A common point among them was they were all earnest in their prayers, and added to this their speeches were praised for always being interesting, marked with tears, and inspirational. Some of those pastors would take a conducting baton from their pockets, begin to sing praise songs, and dance around the stage. As in the olden times of Japan there were Fusidan Speeches made in the temples to gather the people, in Korea there was this kind of charismatic speaker for the church. This kind of new aspect appeared in the 1970s and also has some relationship to the explosion in the numbers of church members.

Section 4 Quiet Revolution (1980s)

Because church growth in the 1970s was so sudden, some members in Korean churches began to wonder about when this growth might stop. However, when we look back now at the time period of the 1980s, the growth of the 1970s that was seen before was not a onetime event.

I think when you measure the power of the growth of a country it is not only industrial power which is visible that should be measured but also the power of people's minds that were behind it. This is because people work by their minds. After World War II there were earth-shaking changes. This means that the number of Christians was growing among Korean leaders who placed Jesus at the forefront of their minds and based their thinking on Christian ideals. When you think about the relationship between Japan and Korea moving forward from today, this fact is very important, but I think in Japan there are too few people who clearly understand this point correctly. The core of this issue is the difference in the views of religion. I am sorry to say there are many Japanese who do not think religion is an important issue. Let's take a look at an example. A Japanese businessman casually asked to a Korean businessman, "Let's go play golf on Sunday?" This is seen as causing an inconsiderate conflict for them, but Japanese businessmen do not understand what the conflict is.

In Korea there are still hard feelings expressed in the sad Arirang song, but the country has completely changed. The atmosphere is filled with self-confidence, cheerfulness, and optimism. The hymns being sang in Korean churches are not only translated hymns from foreign countries, but the opposite is also true with the appearance of Korean composed hymns being exported abroad. The hymn "Sarang ("Love") " was composed by Jeong DooYeong. This hymn is based on scripture from the Bible, and when I heard this hymn, I felt something special which I had never felt before.

Love is patient and Love is kind 사랑은 언제나 오래 참고, 사랑은 언제나 온유하며

Love has no jealousy, conceit or pride, 사랑은 시기하지 않으며, 자랑도 교만도 아니하며

Love is not ill-mannered, selfish, or irritable, 사랑은 무례히 행치않고, 자기의 유익을 구치않고

Love does not keep a record of wrongs. Love is happy with the truth. 사랑은 성내지 아니하며, 진리와 함께 기뻐하네

(This is based on 1st Corinthians Chapter 13 beginning from Verse 4.)

The impression is completely different from the Arirang song, and the melody is new and like chanson. This was totally different from the view of hymns which I had before, but in a strange way this was matching with scriptures from the Bible which are known to every Christian. It evokes the feeling that Korea is also culturally being reborn. In Japan there are many people who see Korea as still being a country of the old way of Confucianism, but actually that is the Korea of the past. Their optimistic and positive attitude which they didn't have before has been greatly influenced by their victory of becoming democratic and the increase in number of Christians during the 1980s.

The Democratization

The political situation in the 1980s in Korea was the age commonly called "the democratization". In opposition to a military regime which had ruled the government for a long time, people recalled the independent movement of "Sam-Il" and fought for a change to a democratic society. The KwangJu Incident of 1980 (광주사태 : A demonstration of young people in the city of KwangJu who were requesting democracy where 189 protesters were killed by the military) was a major incident in modern Korean history. Then in 1987, President Noh TaeWoo (노태우 魯泰愚) made a declaration of democratization and the military regime was finally finished. This declaration is an historical event in Korea and comparable to the Declaration of Independence in America. At that point, Korea announced to their people and to the world that in the manner of a revolution through their own power and sacrifice they had earned democracy and a new beginning was underway. There are also very few Japanese who completely understand the significance of these events.

After World War II the democratization in Japan made progress as a system. In other words, the system of democratization established through GHQ was carried out and developed step by step. On the other hand, the democratic movement in Korea progressed as a movement of society. That is to say, the democratization of Korea was earned by the blood of the people as independence had been by the Sam-Il Movement against the Japanese Colonization and the KwangJu Incident of this era as it is in a revolution of western society.

Among the leaders of this move for democratization there were many Catholic and Protestant Christians and sometimes they were the main leaders of this movement. That is, Pastors and Fathers were standing on the frontline of the battle and also being intellectual supporters. This also resulted in Christianity earning the people's trust.

At its foundation the church has been outspoken in influencing social matters which stems from ethics and philosophy based on Christianity. The real ruler of this world is God, and from this rule, theo ogical philosophy spreads the idea of justice which is flowing from God's love. In Korean churches this following scripture is often recited:

Instead, let justice flow like a stream, and righteousness like a river that never goes dry. (Amos 5:24)

Politics always comes together with compromise and secret agreements. Regarding this point, Japan and Korea has no difference. However, going forward from now, Korea is moving more towards justice in the manner of western society. That is a higher priority is given to seeking justice rather than compromise. Furthermore, the ideal of seeking justice is built upon the theory that humans are weak and sinful and that in any case the priority at all times should be to save those who cannot save themselves. I think the cause of Japanese people or politicians struggling to comprehend Korea might be because they have not paid enough attention or any attention to this religious change there.

From the theory of growing stronger than Japan to the theory of being friends with Japan

In 1982 Korean President Jeon DooHwan (전두환 全斗煥) said in a speech on Independence Day, the memorial day of when World War II ended, "The only way to surely guarantee we will no more experience the hardships or insults of being ruled by another race is for us to make a rich and strong country which is living better than the country who ruled us." This speech was in response to the Japanese textbook screening and approval system by the Japanese government which changed the word "attacked" to "went in" in Japanese history books in reference to Japan's actions against Korea before the start of the Japanese Colonization period. Due to this, the President offered this theory as the only way for surpassing Japan and becoming a powerful country.

However, not everyone in the Korean church was in agreement with this theory. The theory of growing stronger than Japan sounds a little softer than being against Japan, but it is still seen by other countries as an impolite expression so most of the people in Korean churches were even hesitant to use these words very much. There is no specific theory of fellowship, but Korean church people think they should build a relationship of friendship with all other countries including Japan. In Japan, people understand this way to mean to forget about the past and look forward to the future, but this is not such a simple matter. Koreans think that being a broadminded person is a virtue, so the Japanese need to understand that way is a part of the broadmindedness of one who is waiting for another to express regret. This is because no one can just let go of this kind of unforgettable past.

After that speech, President Jeon DooHwan called for an Independence Memorial Hall to be built to house exhibits about the things that occurred during the colonization period of Japan in order to accurately depict the history of what had happened. He asked people to donate funds to build it, and very quickly in the next year in 1983 a ceremony was held to commemorate the beginning of construction, and the Independence Memorial Hall in CheonAn was opened in 1987. The Hall contains very realistic displays and images of the torture and oppression by the Japanese Army of the Colonization Era. When Koreans think about Japan, they recall this period of 36 years of colonial, military, and inhumane rule. After all, how many Japanese truly know about this? Young people today know almost nothing of this, and most Japanese also are not considering these kinds of historical events much. Because Korean young people are educated about this kind of history, these are well-known historical facts. Moving forward from now, Japanese young people need to learn the history of what their own country has done.

An unchangeable sense of values in a society of overwhelming change

In the 1980s the Korean economy experienced sudden and great growth. The GDP per capita in 1980 was US $1,645.00, but in 1990 it grew to US $6,147.00 a growth of 3.7 times in a ten year period. When comparing that to 1970, that reflected a growth of 24 times over a period of 20 years. In 1988 the Seoul Olympics were held. The urban population reached 70% of the total population. Within barely 20 years the country which had been counted among one of the poorest in the world was now standing shoulder to shoulder with developed countries and the world called Korea an example of economic excellence. The term "middle class" also came into popular use in the 1980s. Travel abroad was also freely occurring.

The change of many matters in society also falls into this period of 10 years. Modernization progressed in the countryside with use of machines for planting rice becoming commonplace along with the use of weed killers and the redeployment of arable land. Only elders and children remained in the countryside with many parents moving to urban areas to find work. Even fishermen on the coast began to eat rice. Sea urchin also began to be exported to Japan as an expensive delicacy, and aquaculture began for raising laver. Eating Japanese dishes became very popular. Bridges were built between the mainland and many islands along the coast, and travel to the city as a day trip became commonplace. All of these overwhelming changes occurred during the 1980s.

In the countryside on the islands people also had electric refrigeration. Soon even on the small islands everyone had televisions. Confucian family ceremonies became simplified. People in the countryside stopped holding wedding ceremonies at the family homes and moved them to wedding halls in the city. Burial ceremonies also changed with more people choosing cremation over burial in tombs. The foundation of MoonJung of gathering for and worshipping ancestors is based on Confucian thinking of filial piety, and this also seemed to become less emphasized.

Many people became wealthy, but some people were left out. In the 1980s there were more than 200 poverty stricken slums in Seoul City. In the presidential elections of 1987, most of the people in these areas gave their support to Kim DaeJung (김대중 金大中).

At this time an imbalance developed. In the 1980s the number of girls entering high school rapidly increased and many new high schools were opened. At almost the same time people felt the number of girls entering middle school was so low, now the number of girls entering high school greatly increased. Because of this difference, we can see how drastic the change was which occurred over such a short period of time. At the same time the children of the baby boom were growing up and the number of newborns was drastically decreased. In the 1960s the population growth rate (birthrate) was 2.7%, but barely 15 years later in 1975 the population growth rate (birthrate) dropped to 1.9%. This is the result of a government family plan campaign which reached every corner of the country, and this caused the declining birthrate problem. At the same time the number of elderly began to increase. The 1980s was an age with this kind of drastic change in society. Furthermore, in the 1980s, the world was experiencing an IT (Internet Technology) revolution.

During this kind of drastic change in society, the numbers of Protestant Christians continued to increase. From this kind of situation, to see the increase in numbers of Christians as only coming from the changes in society is incorrect as it is only a part of the reason for the growth. There are many examples where society greatly changed but the religion of the country still did not change. The changes in society in Korea were only secondary factors which influenced the number of Christians increasing. The primary catalyst for the increase in the number of Christians in Korea was religious and the movement of belief.

If you have a situation where the economic environment is greatly improved, it is easy for people to be confused about their sense of values. However in this case the Korean church and society grew at the same time which is one of the core reasons behind the explosion of numbers of Christians in Korea.

An increase of 8,600,000 in 20 years (Protestant believers)

I already mentioned the first time Protestant Christianity entered Korea was through the large sects of the Methodist and Presbyterian Church. These missionaries arrived in Korea on the same ship, and they often joke about which was the first to actually step out from the ship onto the land of Korea. This is a way of talking time-wise about which is one step ahead of the other. These two groups continue to be the largest groups of Christian churches in Korea.

To these groups was added the Holiness Union which has a large following and they are called the Big Three Groups of Korean Protestant Churches. Another group that is becoming well-known in Korea is the Assembly of God Church which places emphasis on spiritual experience and has been growing since the end of World War II. Besides these there are more than 100 small groups such as Baptist, Anglican Church and the Salvation Army. All of these groups have increased their numbers of believers:

1970s 3,200,000 (percentage of total population is 10%)

1980s 7,200,000 (percentage of total population is 19%, an increase of 4,000,000 in 10 years)

1990s 11,880,000 (percentage of total population is 30%, an increase of 4,680,000 in 10 years)

As illustrated in this data, for the 20 years from 1970 to 1990 the increase of 8,600,000 of Korean Protestant Church believers was tremendous. I call this the "Quiet Revolution" of Korea. The optimism that sprang from the successful democratization and the growth of Christianity led Korea to become a new country. The point I most want correctly understand Korea.ferfCharlottesermon and brightly and enthusiastically singing hymns and praying,133 appealing to many people, and in Korea after World War II the number of Catholic believers favorably increased. Of course, behind this there is also the influence of the extraordinary martyrdoms. However because the increase in Protestant believers was so noticeable, this increase in Catholic believers garnered very little attention. Yet since the 1980s the Catholic Church in Korea started to rapidly grow. In 1980 Catholics numbered 1,400,000, but in 1990 the number had risen to 2,400,000.

In the 1980s the most noticeable thing that happened in the Catholic Church in Korea was that Pope John Paul II visited. In 1984 the Korean Catholic Church began the 200th year memorial of the beginning of Catholic missions, and the Pope visited Korea. At that time 1,000,000 Catholic believers filled YeoUiDo Park. In the church history, the Catholic Church began their missions in Korea one hundred years prior to when the Protestant Church missionaries came, and with this event of the Pope coming to Korea, the numbers of Catholic believers in Korea noticeably increased.

Protestant and Catholic Church believers in 1990 combined to number over 14,000,000 people. This is 35.7% of the total population (40,000,000). It was reported at the time that the numbers of Buddhist believers accounted for about 23% of the population, but this could not be a realistic number. Because when counting the number of Christians, the numbers came from the number of attendees who had been baptized and were attending public services such as worship and contributing to the offerings at each church which are reported to their main association offices, so that data is fairly accurate. The Buddhist number is however counted in a fashion very similar to the way it is in Japan, and that method is very ambiguous. Moreover, about half of the people do not have a specified religion. In this way in the 1980s, Christianity was the largest religion in Korea in name and in actuality.

In this manner the Catholic and Protestant Church continued to progress, and there are many episodes which Japanese people have difficulty understanding or things which easily cause misunderstandings. I will introduce several of these which will help (Japanese) people to more easily understand the passionate mind of belief and Korean ethnic character.

The passion of believers

In a small church in Seoul city there was a devoted GweonSa (권사 勸 士 : female church elder and helper). She lived in a small house and definitely was not wealthy. She was an enthusiastic church member who was attending Morning Prayer Meeting daily.

This church had a long time dream to build a new and magnificent big church building. This goal was openly discussed and when the pastor set forth a specific plan to the church attendees for attaining it, she pledged to donate 5,000,000 Won. However, she was soon diagnosed with a terminal illness and was hospitalized. Then she told her son about her pledge to donate 5,000,000 Won, but her son immediately offered 10,000,000 Won. This episode shows a son's love for his mother and the single-mindedness of the character of Korean men.

Another man using his house as collateral donated money he received from a loan from the bank for building the new church. Another story tells of a woman who cut and sold her hair and donated the proceeds for the church building fund. Of course these were not things the church encouraged or recommended. These show the pureness or single-mindedness of Koreans. Of course, these are special stories and not every Korean Christian is like this.

There was a person we will call "Attendee A". His business was failing and he had fallen very ill. He was forced to live with his wife and 3 children in a single room without even a kitchen. At the time he was experiencing this, the pastor announced to attendees that the next Sunday a special service would be held for inviting new members to church. Each church elder was assigned to invite 100 people. Each deacon was assigned to invite 70 people, and regular attendees were given the goal of inviting 50 non-Christians. "Attendee A" boldly announced he would invite 2000 people. Then he visited and invited everyone he knew to come; people who were in the jewelry business like he was, also relatives, people who lived in his village, friends, alumnus of his school, wives of the shop owners he regularly visited, people from beauty and hair shops, a cosmetics saleslady, newspaper delivery people, and the customers who visited his shop. He did not quite reach 2000 people but the total was 1051 who he invited. Among them there was a fortune teller and "Attendee A" persuaded that person to come by saying he could come just one time. Soon he gave up being a fortune teller and was converted to Christianity.

In Korea this kind of special service meeting has an atmosphere filled with the passion of every believer. Some people say this looks like a spiritual party.

After that meeting "Attendee A" was miraculously healed of the cholecystitis, severe inflammation of the gallbladder, his business suddenly began to prosper, he was able to move into a large apartment with 3 bedrooms, and now lives in a 3-story home. (20)

The burgeoning growth in the numbers of Protestant believers in Korea from 1970 to 1990 was carried along by the passion of these kinds of believers.

After finishing his breakfast quickly, taking with him every child from his village one ten year old boy went to the church in a neighboring village 2 kilometers away. Several weeks later those children who were guided there by the boy before could now find their way on their own. Japanese children differ from others by their character of following rules well, but Korean children have a character that is marked by being allowed to make their own decisions about many things. Endlessly being told by their upper classmen at school to attend church is not considered appropriate, and they are choosing to attend church of their own free will. It could happen that Korean children's autonomy comes from Confucianism. This autonomy is a trait of their ethnic character and another of the reasons for the great growth of the numbers of Christians in Korea.

The life of Christian believers

"Person B" grew up in Incheon City where there is the largest international airport in Korea. For now, Incheon City has become the 3rd largest city in South Korea behind Seoul and Busan. In 2008 the populations of several large cities were as follows:

Seoul City	10,030,000
Busan City	3,500,000
Incheon City	2,630,000
Daegu City	2,450,000

Even though family and friends made invitations to church, "Person B" did not show any interest in attending. In 1987, when "Person B" turned 20 years old, a brother died due to illness, so a pastor came and performed the funeral ceremony. After all, this resulted in "Person B" voluntarily attending church. For about the first six weeks, he received an introductory education from an associate pastor before every Sunday service. After that, for about 6 months, he was taught for about an hour each week progressing up through the levels of studies. Upon completion of that study, he received instruction about preparing for baptism, and when that finished he was formally baptized. This example of "Person B" is a common example of how a person in Korea becomes a Christian.

I think Protestant believers in Korea view changing churches positively. In Japan, the names of believers are on the rolls of the churches to which they belong. In other words, Japanese have their names recorded there, so they are not considering changing their church lightly. On the other hand, for Koreans the church they are attending is usually considered as their church. It means Koreans place no importance on the record keeping system of the Japanese church. Koreans think to quit a church that does not fit with their belief and to move to another church is seen as a more honest way to live. With this reasoning, Korean Christians are moving to different churches more freely than Japanese Christians.

The rapid increase in the number of emigrants

There are many Koreans who are living abroad. In 1965 the immigration laws in America changed and the number of people who emigrated from Korea to America reached its peak in the 1980s. In 1970 there were barely 40,000 Koreans living in Hawaii and the western portion of the continental U.S. But 15 years later in 1985 that number reached 1,000,000 and made up the largest Asian population in the U.S. It is more suitable to express this as an explosive increase than it is to say it was just a rapid increase.

Normally those people who were immigrating to America were people who were low-income families in their home countries, yet 60% of Korean immigrants were college graduates or in other words people from the middle class. 65% of those immigrants were Christians, and there were many who converted to Christianity after immigrating there. Therefore about 80% of the Korean immigrant population is Christian.

Emigrating was not only to America. Koreans were proceeding to enter countries all around the world. There are many people who went to Saudi Arabia to earn money or countries on the coast of the Mediterranean Sea. In Japan it is often said that if you visit any country in the world you will find Japanese people, but from this time the number of Koreans who have emigrated has rapidly increased and now is far more than the number of Japanese emigrants. Anywhere in the world you can meet more Koreans than Japanese. The lives of people from any race who emigrates would have their difficulties, but Koreans built their own communities surrounding their churches and help each other.

Military duty and Christianity

Korea still exists under the armistice agreement with North Korea. Presently there also exists the situation of living under the tension of wondering when an attack from North Korea might occur. Actually, in November of 2010, there was a sudden attack by North Korea on YeonPyeong Island in the north western part of South Korea that resulted in civilian casualties. This means that at this moment Korea is still under a war-like condition. For this reason, after the Armistice Agreement military duty is required of all men older than 19 years of age.

Normally they are training and serving for about 2 years after graduating high school or while taking a break from university after their second year of studies. This term was almost 3 years before, but little by little it has been shortened over time and it has been announced that in 2014 it will be shortened to about 1 and a half years. Half of the nation has made up their mind to do this for their country, and 60% feel it is a positive experience for them.

When attending that military duty, the first six weeks are for basic training and afterwards they are sent to their individual troops to finish out their service. Of course there are some breaks with those 2 years of hard life with their troops. Their life is rising every morning at 6:00, attending muster and roll call, running while chanting military songs, eating breakfast and then attending daily education and training, and of course often performing military drills. The government is providing their food and clothing along with a stipend.

Sunday is basically an off day, but if you have no plans you will be assigned some tasks, so going outdoors to play sports or attending church services is common. Many soldiers are attending church services on Sunday. In the 1980s 40% of enlisted men and 70% of officers were Christians. If you attend church, there are many education programs prepared. Among the many young soldiers who are doing their military duty, 2000 to 3000 were baptized every week. Of course there are Buddhist activities as well, so not only Christian activities were available. However, religious activities in the military mostly consist of Christian activities.

The case of campus missions

Young people mostly are connected to Christianity by invitation of their peers and friends. In Korea, campus missions for high school and college students are very prominent and popular. Most high schools and colleges in Japan forbid religious activity on their campuses or watch over activities very closely. This is because in Japan there are many religions which have caused problems in society by doing things such as mind control or selling bogus expensive religious talismans. There are many parents who do not wish for their children to be strongly connected to any type of religion, and you can say that the underlying cause is a non-religious society with more of a focus on materialism and mammonism in Japan spreading after World War II. Of course in Korea there are also several questionable religions who are recruiting high school and college students. However, real education should be to teach students to distinguish for themselves which of those should be considered as legitimate. Campus missions have the responsibility for covering this area of a student's education.

There are several organizations that specialize in campus missions. Those organizations pay to send young specialists for missions on campus and to provide activities to continue educating the students there about Christianity. For example there is CCC, Campus Crusade for Christ, in Korea. In 1984 this association paid to send 130 missionaries to campuses all over and 10,000 students volunteered with them and participated in their activities.

Among the associations for campus missions worldwide, many are started abroad and mainly from America, but the difference for campus missions in Korea is that several of the associations were started there. University Bible Friendship Association (대학성서친교회 大学聖書親交会) in Korea was started in 1961, and since 1974 there activities have spread to America, Germany, Bangladesh, Brazil, Japan, Canada and several other countries.

In Korea in 1986 missions in elementary, middle, high school, and colleges were thriving. In that year, 30% of teachers of elementary through high school and 25% of college professors were Christian. For now this kind of tendency is still growing stronger. Students were being converted to Christianity while they were young then becoming teachers and growing into a national power. The influence of this kind of education will bring major changes to Korean society from now and going forward. Deriving an image of youth in Korea from only watching Korean television dramas or the music scene such as K-Pop would result in an incorrect view.

Christianity in Korean Society

With the increase in the number of Christian believers there is a greater percentage of local and national government officials who are Christian. More Christian officials show that Christians think that their ideals have meaning in actual practice in society in general.

I mentioned before about Christianity having a strong influence on official education and social services. The increase in the numbers of Christian believers in the 1980s made apparent on the surface the power of the influence of Christianity which had previously been mostly an underlying influence. This means that Christianity became a recognizable part of Korean society.

An explosion in the number of Christians has the possibility of causing many societal problems. This is not only limited to Christianity. A rapid increase in the number of believers in any religion could raise red flags to believers of other religions.

Regarding this point, the question was asked of all 26 Protestant Church leaders in my survey. The results were 14, more than half, that people accepted this occurrence positively. 8 people answered that it caused a guarded reaction. 4 people answered they had various other responses. Among the varied responses there was one who answered that "at that time I was still a child, so I don't know". This person is among the leaders who were in their 30s, and now more than twenty years have passed since the period of the explosion in believers in the 1980s. The reasons for those who answered the change was positively accepted was because there were many believers in history who sacrificed themselves in devotion to their country and many people who trusted Christianity which taught that people should love others and had performed many charitable works.

The reasons behind the explosion in Christian believers in the 1980s as seen by Korean pastors

The explosion of Christian believers in Korea which began in the 1970s became without doubt well-known around the world and many foreign researchers began to visit Korea for researching and studying this. As for Japan, pastors visited for observing this, but researchers, journalists, and economists mostly paid little attention to it. This might have been because to Japanese people it was not easy to understand the meaning this kind of religious change might bring for a country.

The average attendance for Sunday services during the year of March 1980 to March of 1990 for GwangLim Methodist Church in Seoul City increased more than 2 times from 1502 to 3500. The pastor of this church, Kim SeonDo, wrote in the appendix of his dissertation which was presented in 1983 nine reasons for the explosion of the numbers of Protestant believers. Those reasons were as follows:

1. Fervent prayer such as that which was held in almost every church every morning during Morning Prayer Meeting and every Friday holding Evening Prayer Meeting brought this about. Those people of the Korean Protestant church who did not know how to grow their church just prayed earnestly about it in this fashion.
2. The Korean church educated their people about the Bible and believers memorized bible scriptures.
3. Actual works by the Holy Spirit were prominent and many spiritual meetings were held (services or Bible study)
4. The blood of martyrdom and of those severely persecuted during the time of the Japanese Colonization played an important role. The persecution and suffering brought by the Communists of the Korean War also played a role.
5. Believers tithed ten percent of their income.
6. Koreans have deeply religious minds. This was seen before from the worship of their ancestors and in shamanistic ceremonies.
7. The Korean church leaders are well-trained believers and perform

143

required church work or missions.

8. Korean churches create many smaller groups within the church and study the Bible or perform mission activities.

9. The move to becoming an urban society also played a role in the explosion. In the 20th century worldwide urbanization increased, and in Korea this had a positive effect and impacted the increase in the numbers of Christian believers.

Section 5 Sprouting of the seed (1990s)

The Slowing of the Protestant Church membership increase

In the mid-1990s the increase in the number of Protestant believers began to taper off. In 1990 the number of Protestant Christian believers was 11,880,000. This is almost the same as in 2000 when the number was 12,000,000. When considering the increase, the term lasted for about 20 years, the urban population now was stable, and the percentage of increase in the past was too rapid, so this can be seen as now falling into a term of adjusting. To get a picture of the church at that time, think of a church which is just outside Seoul City.

Presently that city is called GoYang City, but before it was a small country village in the countryside west of Seoul City. In the late 1980s that area began to develop. The church being referred to here also was included in this development. After only about 4 years of growth from 1989 to 1993, GoYang City changed to a modern housing town with tall apartments springing up like a forest and standing where rice fields once had been.

From earlier a Presbyterian Church was established there. This church also moved to a better location and changed from a country church to a city church. This church started as small country church in the 1930s during the Japanese Colonization Era and had about 80 people attending. Because of the move, in 1992 attendance dropped to about 40. After the move was completed in 1995 attendance surged to 300. In 1996 attendance was 600, and in 1999 it was more than one thousand.

However, those church elders' who made up the council for deciding about things regarding every aspect of church management came from the original group of church members and there were only 5. The church elders basically serve for all of their lives, so the development of new believers being selected as church elders is being delayed. This resulted in the fact that the things voted on and passed in the full membership meetings was often vetoed or not approved by the council, so this caused conflict with the 1000 member congregation not always agreeing with the council which had only a few members. After all, the number of believers dropped off to about 900 and membership growth came to a stop.

This is the same as in any country in the world that while there are some big churches there are also small churches gathering with only a few members. In Korea also there are Mega Churches and there are small churches surviving by borrowing a room in a building and gathering with 20 or 30 people. The membership numbers are different, but the contents and core activities are basically the same. All of them are called "church". This means that among churches there is no hierarchy or good and bad. Believers attend the church they like going to. The Protestant Church manages church considering the voice of all members, so the kind of problem I previously mentioned more or less occurs in all churches.

The great movement of the Catholic Church

The number of believers in the Catholic Church in 1990 was 2,300,000. In the year 2000, this number jumped to 4,070,000. The number of attendees at Mass nearly doubled at all the Catholic churches during this 10 year period. This means that just as the explosion of Protestant believers had finished, the explosion of Catholic believers began. However, for the 10 years of 1990 to 2000 the total population increase was also high, so while the Christian population increased, the overall percentage decreased only slightly from 35.7% to 34.6%.

This explosion in Catholic believers was based on the blood of tens of thousands of Catholic martyrs of the past. As Father Tertullianus said, we should not forget their blood was the seed which was planted in the minds of the Korea people.

The Catholic Church did not stand against the Confucian beliefs of worshipping ancestors as the Protestant Church did, and did not strictly forbid use of alcohol and tobacco. It might be that this kind of attitude was acceptable to many people. The Catholic Church was also passionate about social work and supported the development of farmers' lives and establishing workers' rights. These ideas also were very appealing to many people.

This story is a little old, but the Catholic Church held their world meeting from 1962 to 1965 and at that meeting the modernization of the Catholic Church in the world began with things like using the native language of a country in church services, started giving believers greater membership roles, and performing missions taking into consideration the different situations of each country. However, the Catholic system reaches all over the world, so it took a long time for these changes to reach all corners and being put into actuality. Another of the reasons for the explosion in numbers of Catholic believers in Korea was the influence of those decisions was only just now reaching Korea.

They were also influenced by Mother Theresa (1910-1997). She earned a Nobel Peace Prize in 1979. Her works after that spread worldwide. Her attitude as a witness of God's love was singled-mindedly to serve the needy moved the hearts of people all over the world. This is also one of the reasons which contributed to Korean people entering the Catholic Church.

There is another reason for the great growth in Catholic believers. Some people converted from the Protestant Church. This reason was named in a research paper titled "Korean Religious Character As Seen Through Converters"(Korea, published by Shepherds Sociology Research Center written by two Protestant professors, Jeong JaeYeong (실천신학대학원 実践神学大学院 : Graduate School of Practical Theology) and Yi

SoonHoon (한림대학교 翰林大学校 : *Hallym University*). They state that those people were converted to the Catholic Church due to preferring calm and quiet services rather than the Protestant Church which was filled with many activities.

Until the collapse of the JoSeon Dynasty, Korea was a country which surely held Confucianism as its national religion. This lasted until 1910. For the following 80 years and nearing the last of the 20th century was a term that included the colonization era, Korea changed slowly, but greatly, from a country which had Confucian ideals to a country with Christian ideals. It became a nation where every week one third of the population attended Catholic or Protestant Church services. It is no small thing they continued to be educated in the ways of the Bible. This greatly influences culture, education, economy, politics, diplomacy, and more. We Japanese need to pay attention to this point.

Sudden modernization

Entering the 1990s new changes were taking place in Korea. As Japan had experienced, in the countryside there were fewer and fewer young people to be successors and the areas were becoming deserted and changed to a sparsely populated and aged society. People continued moving into the city and one by one elementary schools in the countryside closed. In 1990 the Uruguay Round made the decision to establish an open market for grain, and maintaining an agricultural life in Korea became more difficult. The middle-class in urban society increased more and more. Seoul City area and Busan City area became overpopulated and soon overflowed.

In 1991 a law for developing and promoting agriculture and aquaculture was enacted, and kitchens and toilets in the countryside were modernized. In the city, karaoke became popular and every house had a modern kitchen facility. Accordingly the number of cars grew exponentially and many gas stations appeared. The number of registered cars in 1970 was only 130,000, but by 1980 this number had increased to 770,000 and by 1990 ballooned to 4,800,000. Moreover, in 2000 this number reached almost 14,000,000. Korea also became a car society as had Japan. The area of the nation is very narrow, so if there is no traffic congestion it is possible to travel the whole country roundtrip in one day.

GNP per capita in 1990 was US $6,308, and in 2000 reached US $11,347. Within a ten year period it had increased 1.8 times. Korea entered the age of high tech industry. People's lives were getting enriched but at the same time it was occurring disproportionately. Along with this the societal gap also grew bigger. The change was especially great in Seoul and Busan. In Europe it took about one hundred years for modernization to occur, but Japan did it in half the time with 50 years. Korea only took 30 years. The progress in the Korean economy and society for the 30 years from 1970 to 2000 was that great. At the same time the disproportionate distribution of wealth and social gap grew larger as well. In this time period the number of Christians was exploding.

The wave of globalization

In the modern age around the globe there is a population of around 7 Billion with around 200 recognized countries. Ethnic groups number about 600. If they were divided more precisely, the number would be more than 2000. Ethnic group division is based on differences in cultural tradition. In other words, countries with several ethnic groups are becoming commonplace. Many Koreans are working abroad while on the other hand many foreigners are living in Korea. The situation is the same for Japan. Every country in the world is in the process of becoming a multi-ethnic country.

There have been some Korean students studying abroad since before

World War II, but these days the numbers have greatly increased. I already described the situation where after World War II many Koreans emigrated. That number has also greatly increased in recent years. Since the 1980s, the number of Koreans who have also been going abroad to many different countries to find migrant work has also risen sharply. The rise is a trend of the ages which started not too long ago and began in full in the 1990s. Koreans working abroad have gained the reputation of being good workers.

In the same period of the 1990s, Koreans were sometimes called "ugly Koreans" by foreigners. In American society, Koreans entering society became noticeable in the 1980s. In 1992 there was an incident in Los Angeles where members of a different ethnic group attacked a Korean shop which was among several shops which had suddenly began to prosper in the area. The Korean Americans fought back with guns. Compared to many other groups of ethnic Americans, Korean Americans have a stronger sense of the need to defend themselves. This comes from the cruel history of the Japanese Colonization which they experienced. The scene of Asians fighting back with guns was shown across the country on television and shocked a nation which was made up of so many different ethnic groups. After that occurred, a church intervened and acted as intermediary and put an end to the fighting by performing a ceremony demonstrating humility, and they said people from different ethnic groups should co-exist with understanding and acceptance as was depicted in the Bible with Jesus washing the feet of the disciples.

On the other hand, domestically in Korea in 1995 there was an incident involving foreign workers who staged a protest rally at the MyeongDong Catholic Church in Seoul. Those migrant workers who had come from different countries gathered at the MyeongDong Catholic Church to protest against inhumane treatment by the owners of the companies where they worked. The Catholic Church supported them. This incident demonstrates the economic progress of Korea and the rapid globalization.

Irritation with Japan

Because in 1990 a Japanese official of the Department of Labor stated that Korean women forced to be "Comfort Women" during World War II were done so by private business entities and not by the Japanese government, in 1991 women who had been "Comfort Women" came out publicly and loudly protested. Then in 1992 the Japanese Prime Minister Miyazawa Kiichi visited Korea and apologized. Since that year every Wednesday in front of the Japanese Embassy in Seoul City a demonstration has been held demanding a formal apo ogy and indemnification from the Japanese government. Former comfort women first came out publicly in the mass media since the 1980s which was encouraged by the Korean democratic movement of that time.

When Prime Minister Miyazawa visited Korea, he spoke at the Korean National Assembly, and it was received positively as a good speech. This is because he gave that speech based on historical facts. However, there are still many Japanese politicians and academics who continue to irrationally argue the positives of this event. Some of those arguments are as follows:

- Japan attacked Korea, but they did some good things for Korea, too.
- Considering this historically that war was not one of attacking but an act of self-defense for Japan
- The purpose was to bring Asian countries independence and release from oppression

All of these come from a selfish historical view which does not consider the position and rights of Koreans. It is an undisputable fact that Japan just attacked Korea, and with military force ruled Korea for 36 years which is also a fact, so Japan should accept these facts and apologize. The citizens of Japan also should not ignore this fact and understand the true aspects.

Section 6 Present day Korean churches (2000s)

35.7% of the population is Christian

In 2009 the population of Korea was 48,500,000. (North Korea was 23,530,000, about half the number of South Korea.) The number of Protestant and Catholic believers in 2010 combined is a little more than 17,300,000 and is estimated as 35.7% of the total population. For 20 years from 1990 to 2010, the number of Protestant believers increased by only 220,000. While on the other side, Catholic believers greatly increased by 2,800,000. Due to this the total number of Christians increased greatly. Let's take a look at the current situation of the Protestant and Catholic Church in Korea.

The Protestant Church of the present

According to data from 2010, the number of Protestant churches is a little more than 53,000. The number of believers is about 12,100,000 and about 24.9% of the total population. This means about 1/4th of the people are Protestant believers. These numbers are based on the data released this year (2011) from each church group and association and added to past data from the estimated numbers from other church groups.

The General Assembly of Presbyterian Church in Korea (합동 合同) 2,930,000

The Presbyterian Church of Korea (통합 統合)　　　　2,800,000

The Presbyterian Church in Korea (PCK:Kosin) (고신 高神) 470,000

Methodist　　　　　　　　　　1,580,000　(7,780,000)

Assembly of God	1,500,000
Holiness Church	800,000
Baptist Church	800,000
Others	1,220,000
	12,100,000

"Others" means small sects of Presbyterian churches outside of the main three, The Salvation Army, Anglican Church of Korea, and more than 10 other small groups or single independent churches.

For any country for any religion it is not easy to have 100% accurate data on member numbers, but the number of Protestant believers estimated in Korea as around 12,000,000 is a fairly reliable number. I am expecting more accurate numbers to be released later in someone else's research.

The explosion in the number of Protestant believers began in the 1970s and ended in the 1990s. After that the increase was very slow with just small increases. Because a person's religion usually lasts for their lifetime, a rapid decrease in the number of believers is not likely to happen. With this theory in mind, the number of Protestant believers will be in an adjusting stage for a while and then enter the next stage.

In Korea there are more than 10 mega-churches spread across the country which are Protestant Churches. Attendance is greater than 10,000 people for each. In the case of the MyeongSeong Presbyterian Church in 2010 attendance is 95,000, GwangLim Methodist Church attendance is 60,000 to 70,000, and YeoUiDo SoonBokEum Church Assembly of God has attendance of 1,000,000. One mega-church in a smaller city has a church which seats 18,000, and every Sunday holds chapel services 5 times. The large parking lot is filled with cars and buses coming and going. Often this kind of mega-church is the topic of conversation in places around the world. Among the total number of 53,000 Protestant churches in Korea, most of them are categorized as mid to small-sized churches. There are also many small churches with only around 10 people in attendance.

Christian churches teach awareness to their members about churches and organizations related to Moonism as heresy which promote things such as mass wedding ceremonies. In Japan there are also several heretic groups which started in Korea. Every age has people who pretend to be the coming of Christ and cheat people. Of course the numbers from this kind of group are not included in this data.

The Catholic Church of the present

As of 2010 there are 1,609 Catholic Churches in Korea and 813 Catholic Missions. Catholic churches are part of a large world-wide system, so new churches are part of a strategic plan. The total number of Catholic believers in Korea is 5,205,589 which is 10.7% of the total population (48,500,000). In this way the total number of Christian believers in Korea reaches 35.7% when combining Protestant and Catholic believers.

A university which was started by the Catholic Church is SeoGang

University which is managed by Jesuits and is very famous and comparable to Jyochi University in Japan. MyoungDong Catholic Church was built on the place of the house of the first martyrdom which I described earlier, and it is an important memorial place of the democratic movement. This place is called JeolDuSan and is on the banks of the HanGang River where the sacrifice of martyrs took place which is held very sacred by Catholic believers. A museum is also located there.

Churches around the world in the 21st century

As Pastor Yi SeongBong explained before that "spreading the Gospel was moving onward and onward as water flows onward endlessly..." at this moment Korean churches are also ever moving forward into the unknown. Water is always progressing forward towards its goal. It might mean that they do not even have a clear image of how the progress will take place.

One of the differences found in Korean churches is that about 7,000,000 Koreans are living abroad, so more than 7,000 Korean churches are spread throughout the world. Another difference is that nowadays in 2010 Korea is sending the second most missionaries around the world. First is the U.S, but with the total population in Korea being a little less than 50,000,000 and sending 21,000 missionaries around the world is remarkable. When looking at the expense alone, funding missionaries is very costly. Added to this number are the many Koreans sent as missionaries for short terms to places around the world including Japan with private funds such as students using their school break, and this means the total number would be much greater.

Christian churches around the world continue to change. The globalization which started in the latter part of the 20th Century has started in the church as well, and in the 21st Century it is accelerating.

For example, a Catholic Church in the parish of Oakland, Californian in America is using more than 50 different languages besides English for conducting Mass. This is because there are this many different ethnic groups and races living in this area. In Japan there are Catholic churches with foreigners attending such as Japanese-Brazilians, Peruvian, and Filipino and others in greater numbers than Japanese attendees.

In the Protestant Churches as well there are many new attendees who are evangelicals which emphasize a personal and direct relationship with God and outnumber attendees of traditional denominations such as Presbyterian, Methodist, and Anglican. Furthermore there is a larger number of Christians who are part of the spiritual innovation movement which is connected with aspects such as spiritual healing and having no ties to either Catholics or Protestants.

The lives of Pastors and Catholic Fathers

Churches are supported by the offerings of the attendees. Korean attendees give generously. Christians believe everything in life is given by God, so they make offerings of several percentage points of their income with a thankful heart of their own will. In this way, a large church in Korea with more than 10,000 people attending has an estimated income that equals the budget of a municipal office of a small village. The financial records of the churches are open to the members and it is difficult to find instances of illicit expenditures. Pastors and Catholic Fathers are not responsible for those offerings, and attendees such as church elders or deacons are appointed to oversee that work.

Let me explain here about the salaries for pastors and Catholic Fathers. Not only in Korea, but in any country the lives of pastors and Catholic Fathers are usually very frugal. The Fathers of the Catholic Church are unmarried, so there is no need for expenses other than for their personal needs. Some churches give high salaries (*This is usually not called 'salary' in Korea but called 'SaRye* (사례 謝礼)*' or 'money given in thanks'.*) to their pastors. The salary received by the pastor of a mega-church in Korea is much greater than that provided to pastors of smaller churches. Most pastors are spending frugal or average lives. Except for the money needed for operational fees, churches usually use their funds for supporting social assistance programs or a building program.

Korea becomes a rival of Japan

In 2010 the GDP per capita in Japan was US $42,325 while it was US $20,165 for Korea. In 2000 it was US $36,800 in Japan and US $11,347 in Korea, so in this ten year period Korea reduced the gap between them and Japan. According to the book titled "World Data White Papers 2011" (published by Kimoto Publishing) the ranking of Global Competitiveness places Japan in 6th and Korea at 22nd, but when comparing the specific areas such as Business Sophistication, Japan places 1st and Korea 24th, in Innovation Japan ranks 4th and Korea 12th. However in the area of Macro-economy, Korea ranks 6th and Japan 10th, and in Technological Readiness, Korea ranks 19th and Japan is 28th. Products for export from Korea are machines, cars, electronics, ships, refined oil products, and precision instruments, and all of these are in direct competition with Japanese made products. Each side has their own areas of excellence, but economically Korea is in competition with Japan.

With the growth in economy some negative aspects also appeared. The ideology of materialism became a part of Korean thinking. There is more crime and the problems of decreasing birthrate and rapidly increasing elderly population. The suicide rate in 2005 per 100,000 people reached

21.9 (In Japan it was 23.7).

In Korea regionalism is very strong. For example it would be like if Aichi Prefecture and Shizuoka Prefecture would show their competitive side with any little thing that arises. However, there is not this kind of thinking in Japan. Moreover, the difficulty of competition to enter prestigious universities continues, major companies dominate recruitment of promising young people, there are problems caused by maintaining separation of people based on social hierarchy, and discrimination between men and women still exists. The occurrence of appointments of former political or government officials to important posts after retirement is higher than that of Japan. There is "Test Sickness" which is the illness caused by the stress of being overly anxious about passing the Bar Exam. There is also discrimination based on which school someone graduated from along with discrimination based on economic situations, and the situation grows worse and worse with the gaps widening.

In Japan these topics of the negative points of Korea are often talked about, but why isn't the topic of religion, which is the biggest change and the principle that controls the actions and thinking of Korea, discussed? I think this is because Japanese do not place much importance on religion.

The "Hallyu (한류 韓流)" Boom

In 2003 there was something new that happened between Korea and Japan. The Korean TV drama "Winter Sonata" was broadcast in Japan and started a craze. This is called "Hallyu Boom", and it caused a major shift in the way Japanese think of Koreans. What made this drama have such an impact especially on middle-aged Japanese women's minds?

For a long time, Japanese placed higher importance on love for their nation or company above their own personal loves. To middle-aged Japanese women who had grown up in this kind of culture, the exotic sense of hearing "I love you" spoken so directly deeply moved them.

Because I grew up after World War II, when I was a child, "love" was a word with a sense of discomfort and was not commonly used like it is these days. The word "love" was simply not a word in daily use in older times in Japan. After I began attending church, I first started to use this word commonly. Korea which has Confucian ideals would be in the same situation as Japan was.

If this is true, I think it might be the Korean drama boom which occurred 40 years after the number of Christians began exploding resulted from a new culture being developed. I heard expressing one's emotions is highly regarded in Korea. It could mean this shows the best part of Korean culture has begun to blossom. Furthermore, since around 2006, for people from their teens to their 30s the music called Korean Pop (K-Pop) has become very popular as well. The number of Japanese who visit Korea also is rapidly increasing. It looks like discrimination and the former prejudice was overcome very simply.

Internationalism

There is a story in the Bible about Peter, a disciple of Jesus, who had a vision (Acts, Chapter 10) where an object like a great sheet the size of Tokyo Dome was bound at the four corners descended to the earth. In it were all kinds of four-footed animals of the earth, wild beasts, creepy things, and birds of the air which were considered common and unclean and Jewish people were forbidden to eat. A voice came to Peter, "Rise, Peter; kill and eat." Peter answered, "Not so, Lord! For I have never eaten anything common or unclean."

Right at that moment a foreigner came to visit Peter. Peter was a pure Jewish man and discriminated against foreigners thinking them unclean. However, that foreigner was also guided by a vision from God to visit Peter. The visions seen by these two people were a revelation by God that there is nothing unclean in this world, so they should overcome the discrimination of races and be accepting of foreigners. From that moment Peter realized foreigners should not be called unclean and began to spread Christianity to other races. In this way, Christianity became an international religion.

In the Bible it is taught to overcome discrimination between races. Many Christians in Korea are praying for Japan and trying to build a mutual friendship without concern for the history of having been so harshly persecuted by them which comes from the new philosophy in Korea based on the Christian majority. Many Korean people have become Christians and place importance on education of families and in schools about accepting internationalism will bring improvement and prosperity to Korea. Just broadcasts which focus on being against Japan or defeating Japan is not the correct way

What kind of changes would there be with this kind of growth in the numbers of Christians

I want to consider what kind of changes might occur in Korea which has such a large number of Christians.

The greatest influence that the Bible has on human beings might be on the understanding of humans. What is a human being really? If human beings are just living under their own power, then for someone who can live like that it is no problem, but the weaker people would be separated out and the world would become a Darwinian jungle. If human beings are sinful and weak so that they live a difficult and short life, the only choice is to help each other and live together. The Bible falls on this side. A country inhabited by many people who have this kind of thinking would look very different. This kind of education is dependent upon religion and would not be the kind given or done by the country, but would be provided diligently by the family day by day.

Human beings also need freedom. Freedom would allow for new things to be created. Cherishing freedom provides the desire to create new things. If freedom is limited, humans lose the desire to do almost everything. In Christianity it is taught if you want to have freedom in the end you have to be free from your sin. In other words, the belief of being released from one's sins is the path to receiving real freedom which is the core teaching of Christianity.

... If you abide in My word...you shall know the truth, and the truth shall make free. (John Chapter 8:31-32)

Since the National Assembly member election in the spring of 2012 and the Presidential election in December of 2012, Koreans who live abroad could take part in the elections through their consulates. In the autumn of 2011 at the Korean church I attend in Japan, officials from the Korean consulate came and made an announcement about Koreans living abroad being able to register and participate in elections, and for 6 days from March 28th to April 2nd in 2012 voting for the election was allowed in the consulate. Do not forget for around one hundred years, there was a struggle to gain this kind of democratic freedom in Korea such as or even more progressive than that of western society. I think this kind of progress in Korean society is widely based on people having been educated by scriptures from the Bible such as "whatever you want man to do to you, do also to them" (Matthew 7:12). Nowadays in Korea there is not only progress in technology but also there has even been a change in religion, so their strength of will has progressed beyond that of western society. When you think of Korea, you need to consider this point.

Christianity in Japan – 0.88% of total population

According to the annual report in 2011 of the Christian Almanac published by the Christian Newspaper Company, there are 1,110,000 Christians in Japan which includes members of all Christian denominations such as Protestants, Catholics, and Orthodox, and this is only 0.88% of the total population. In 1985 the number was 0.42%, but after World War II that number has always been very low. From 2010 to 2012, I was with four Protestant Church researchers who published a report titled *"What made the spread of Christianity not fruitful in Japan"* which came up with the following 3 main reasons:

1. Japanese churches did not teach scriptures from the Bible directly.
2. Japanese pastors and leaders are not fully developed as individuals or as Christians.
3. Japanese, including Christians, have not had to overcome an inferiority complex as island people.(23)

One cannot simply make comparisons between Korean and Japanese churches, but on the following three points, Korean churches are directly opposite of Japanese churches. In Korea the character of religion is pure, pastors and church elders have had to fight long and hard, and their ethnic character makes it easy to accept different things.

Praying for Japan

On the Memorial Day for Independence of March 1st in 2008, I attended with Pastor Kozo Yoshida, the pastor of a Japanese church in Seoul, the 89th Memorial Service of JeAm-Ri Church which I described before where 23 villagers had been executed by fire in the church building. The speaker that day was Pastor Choe SeungII (최승일 崔昇日) a bishop of the Korean Methodist Church of the KyeongGi area. The title of his sermon was "Remember the times past and cry". The message was about God teaching people to love their enemy, we should pray for Japan, however, we should never forget about what took place at this church in the past. I think giving a sermon at this kind cf historical place is difficult for a pastor. I also felt the nearly 200 attendees at the service understood very well even though they sat in silence.

Every year when Memorial Day for Independence comes, Sunday sermons and services in Korean churches are usually focused around that topic. According to the church calendar, the Memorial Day for Independence of March 1st always falls around the time of Lent (The term set aside to memorialize Jesus Christ being crucified on the cross.) Every church in the world talks about Jesus Christ being sacrificed on the cross for the forgiveness of sins for all mankind. It cannot be said of every Korean, but it might be at least 1/3 of all Koreans seriously think and pray about forgiveness for Japan.

Every time I visit Korea many Koreans who are associated with a church say to me, "let's pray for Japan" and pray for Japan and me as a visitor from Japan. Japanese, who were the persecutors, say, "Those are things of the past. Japanese today are not the Japanese of the past but people of today. Let's think about our future." I still feel there is a wide gap between the two sides every time when I visit Korea.

Politics and Religion

I am against mixing religion and politics. The separation of politics and religion is an important facet of cultural heritage that mankind has earned with the shedding of much blood. However, the power of religion and its effect on politics cannot be denied.

Korea has a one-chamber system of government, and in 2010 among the 299 members of the Korean National Assembly, 119 were Christians which is 40%. If you consider the office of president, President Kim YeongSam was a church elder of ChungHyeon Presbyterian Church, the following President, Kim DaeJung, was a member of the Catholic Church, and President Noh MooHyeon (노무현 蘆武鉉) had no specific church affiliation, but President Lee MyeongBak who was elected in 2008 was an elder of SoMang Presbyterian Church. Among the past 4 Korean presidents, 3 of them were Christians.

Korean Christians mostly have a positive opinion of President Lee MyeongBak. The president of their country is a church elder with a sincere belief. Furthermore, in his case, he was working as a parking lot attendant at the church, and everybody there had respect for him and had pride in him that this kind of humble Christian was their president.

In the Korean Presbyterian Church an annual meeting of the entire church membership is held, and though elections for elders are held, it is not uncommon for several years to pass with no one being elected. Without the agreement of 2/3rds of the membership, a person cannot be elected as a church elder. This is not an easy obstacle to overcome. Before being elected as a church elder, a person must diligently attend training meetings for becoming a church elder. Even an absence of only one time is a disqualification for being a candidate for the election. In the case of former President Lee MyeongBak due to the reason of having to go abroad for his work and not being able to attend this training program, his candidacy was delayed. In this way, selecting church elders is a difficult thing, and being a church elder is seen as evidence a person has sincere belief and is unbiased of good character. There is a joke that becoming a church elder is more difficult than becoming president.

You cannot say all Christian politicians have the same political virtues, but one of the differences of political virtues from Christianity is to strongly demand justice which I mentioned before. Another thing is they have an apocalyptic view of the world. An apocalyptic view of the world means having the greatest hope in knowing that God is preparing a new world after the end of this world. This is the theology that it is not this world going forward without hope, but going toward the goal of God's promise of fulfillment. Another way to say this is the theology of God is the origin of hope. This is the source of a practical and positive attitude for every Christian politician which means even though any kind of difficulties may exist forward progress will continue.

Chapter 4 Country power of mentality – the future between Korea and Japan

Starting from late in the JoSeon Dynasty, we have looked over the past 200 years of history of this neighboring country from the viewpoint of the progress of the Christian church. I wrote many things about Christianity, but I beg the pardon of any readers who do not have any interest in Christianity to please forgive me and continue to read. I thought this is an important point which could not be avoided in order to understand Korea, so I wrote of this in detail. Here I will give 3 key aspects about Korea and conclude this writing.

Section 1 A Christian country, Korea

There was no big religious shift in Japan after World War II. I think this is strongly influenced by the religious control of the Tokugawa Era. Even though the neighboring country of Korea experienced feudalistic periods in the same manner as Japan, for the past half-century Korea has undergone earth shaking religious change. Because of Japan not experiencing this kind of great religious or belief shift, Japanese may have not noticed the change in Korea. I wrote this book with the intention of helping more Japanese people to understand the basic change which had occurred in Korea and how great a mental change it was. It is because understanding others is very important for building a good relationship between the two countries.

Japanese and Koreans are in the same way diligent, sincere, hard working, intelligent and very similar. If there is a difference between them it is only from the aspect of the mind. The difference of the mind would bring out the difference in their views on values, life, human beings, the purpose of life, the meaning of death, and reaction to illnesses or misfortunes. These kinds of differences would have further influence on many different aspects such as politics, economy, and culture.

For example, Korean democracy came from a victory reached by the shedding of blood. Japan also earned democracy through bloodshed, but it was of the people sacrificed in war which ended with democracy being quietly established as a societal system for them. Therefore in Japan some feudalistic aspects still remain. In Korea also there is still some influence of a feudalistic society, but democracy has progressed more than in Japan.

When considered strictly only from the view of being a religion, Christianity can be seen as a form of fundamentalism, so from this time Koreans' opinions can be seen as being more distinct and clear than that of Japanese. The religious beliefs of Japanese are basically founded on acquiring their own personal desires, so among ten Japanese people, there would be ten different religious beliefs. Because of this, when some problem arises, a Japanese person would suggest their solution quietly based on this wide variety of points of view. In other words, these days differences of opinions based on their individual beliefs comes out in every kind of situation.

On a Japanese news program in November of 2011 there was a report about the first blind, male primetime news anchor in Korea. He was using his hand for reading the stories in Braille and performed his job the same way as a regular news anchor. It might be the first time in the world this happened in primetime news. This not only serves as great motivation to the physically challenged, but it might also have an effect by this private broadcasting company showing this consideration for a person who was handicapped leading people to think about the need for kindness. I feel that behind taking this kind of chance lays a very strong will to do what is right. I think moving forward this kind of incident might be seen in many different areas. The most basic thing is that we Japanese need to see the fact that Korean society has changed to a mostly Christian society.

It would be so foolish if there is someone in Japan who still holds an inferior view of Koreans. Korea is a wonderful country just like Japan is, and Koreans are a wonderful ethnic group as are Japanese. Surely there was between the two countries the term when Japan colonized Korea, but in their long history both countries still have the relationship of twins where it cannot be said that one is the older brother to the other. Even though there are differences in their character, both countries surely have to continue to build a new relationship as national equals.

Section 2 Building a country founded on strong belief

In the Old Testament there is a person named Abraham. He is the predecessor to the Jews and Arabs. Because of this, Jews, Christians, and Muslims respect him as the father of belief. He lived in the time around 1900BC.

Abraham's home town was in a place named Ur, present day Iraq. For keeping his faith, God, who is called 'Lord' in the Bible, guided him to what is now Israel more than 1000 kilometers from his hometown. This story takes place in the first part of the Bible.

When Abraham heard God's voice commanding him to move, together with his family he quickly departed without knowing his destination. This is a story which shows a decision made from his pure belief. Later the Jews have their own history of scattering everywhere throughout the world without knowing their destination because they have this kind of father. It was not only in order to find food. The power of belief can move people's lives and even a country. At this time also there are 7,000,000 Jews living in every country around the world.

In 2011 around 7,000,000 Koreans were living abroad as immigrants, or for work or study. It is a little strange, but the current number is the same as the number or Jews living around the world. The number of Japanese who are living abroad is around 1,100,000. The total population of Korea is less than half of that of Japan. From these numbers, 7 times more Koreans than Japanese are living abroad. Is it because they cannot find food in Korea? No, it is not. It is because there are many Koreans who respect the thinking of Abraham as their father in their belief. Anywhere you go around the world, it will be a place flowing with milk and honey with God together, and anywhere you die, the destination is the eternal hometown of Jerusalem in heaven. In this world of globalization, Koreans quickly moved abroad because many people have their belief like Abraham and not only because of a passion for their business.

Furthermore, Koreans have a mind which loves their neighbors with all human beings being brothers and the teaching of Christ to be a witness for Christianity to the ends of the earth (Acts 1:8). When Japanese people go abroad for their work, people say "Come back home healthy" with the goal of returning to Japan, but in Korea they are sent off with the words, "Do a good job as a witness for Jesus Christ." No one knows if they will be able to come back or not. This is because no one can know what will happen in a person's life. The hometown in their mind is not their home country but heaven. Even though not every Korean businessman is this same way, we Japanese need to understand that many Koreans have this kind of strong belief and disregard for their own life. As America in the past built their country with the beliefs of the Puritans, Koreans are going to build their country with a Christian mind. This is the second key point.

Section 3 Contributions to the world

There is another famous story about Abraham. When he had already grown old, he had a son to be his heir. God then commanded Abraham to sacrifice his son to Him.

Abraham traveled three days with his son and arrived in present day Jerusalem. On a mountainside he bound his son, and at the moment he was about to sacrifice him to God a voice came from heaven which said, "Do not stretch out your hand against the lad, and do nothing to him; for now I know that you fear God" (Genesis 22:12). This story shows Abraham, who did not withhold even his son, is a person with a pure mind who listens to God's voice above that of man.

Later God actually sacrificed His own son on the cross as redemption for the sins of all humans. In other words, it means that the God of Christianity sacrificed His only son to save mankind. This pure love stems from the pure character of God. I saw the pureness of Abraham in the minds of Korean Christians. The character of pureness is the source of great power for mankind. Christianity in Western Society contributed to modern thinking such as freedom, equality, democracy and preservation of human rights with the progress of theology, but in the process the power of religious pureness of the belief in Jesus Christ slipped away unnoticed. Regarding religious pureness from now forward, the Korean Church might make great contributions in the church and society all around the world. The pureness of the ethnic character of Koreans is the third major point.

Regarding the pureness of Korean people, I might be overestimating. I do not have enough space to talk about this specifically, but in fact I think Japanese people also have this kind of pureness, and going on from now, both of these peoples will build deeper relationships as good friends greater than that of the relationships of the people of any other countries.

On March 11, 2011 in Eastern Japan there was a great disaster, and video of the people who live in the area struck by the disaster orderly going about helping each other amazed people around the world. This was a typical reaction for Japanese people, but it was amazing to foreigners. Japan has "Japanese Virtue". The virtue they have is different between Japan and Korea, but they both need to accept each other and prosper together.

In Korea the worlds of business and politics are deeply connected and have a causal relationship, and there are many problems unique to Korean society such as abuse of power, rampant nepotism, and negative feelings of regionalism. In the same way, when Koreans view Japanese society, they see Japan as also having problems that Japanese themselves have not noticed. However, the important point is not to focus on the negatives and instead learn the positive aspects each has.

In order for Korea and Japan to both prosper, it is more important to have an open mind rather than arguing which side is stronger economically or which society is more culturally advanced. In the Bible, the Disciple Paul teaches as follows: [Everybody] "be kindly affectionate to one another with brotherly love in honor giving preference to one another" (Romans 12:10). Only a humble mind can be the foundation for the prosperity of both nations.

In this book I almost did not mention China at all, but when you consider the long history and cultural heritage which we both have, China being a big brother cannot be denied. Of course, this means China is a big brother and not a parent.

The people of the three countries of Japan, China, and Korea have experienced histories of suffering. In World War II, the country with the greatest losses was China. The number of casualties was greater than the number of Jews lost in Europe, and some data estimates this to be as much as 20,000,000 though the numbers cannot be verified. There were many Chinese people killed without ever even having been officially recognized as existing. Fortunately we can share information freely and raise viewpoints such as human rights and the important of life, and we have entered an age of longer life expectancy and convenient technology. We can create friendships with respectful minds with the consideration of each other even if we are not world equals.

NOTES:

1. Min KyeongBae (민경배 閔庚培) "A History of the Korean Church (韓国キリスト教会史)" Translated by Kim ChungIl (김충일 金忠一), (Shinkyo Press, 1981), P.99.   P19
2. Same, P.109.   P19

3. Same, P.109. "After seeing the martyred Catholic Christians (天主教徒の殉教を見て)",: From the Complete works of Yi GwangSoo: Book 17 (Seoul SamZhoongDang Press, 1962), P.463.   P19

4. Tertullianus (c.160–c.225) "Apologeticus (護教論)" Translated by Ichiro Suzuki: From the Christian Church Father's Works Vol. 14, (KyoBunKan Press, 1987), P.117.-P.118.   P20

5. Ham SeokHeon, (함석헌 咸錫憲 : 1901-1989) "On This Road Till I Die (죽을 때까지 이 걸음으로 死ぬまでこの歩みで)" Translated by Katsuji Kosugi, (Shinkyo Press, 1991), P.181.   P25
6. Samuel Hugh Moffett, *The Christians of Korea* (N.Y.: Friendship Press, 1962), P.58.   P26

7. ZhangHyo, (장효 張暁) "Korean Peoples and Their History (韓国の民族とその歩み)": From the committee for publishing "Korean Peoples and Their History", 1963), P161   P
8. Takeshi Yamamoto (山本剛士) "Introduction of Korea, New Edition (韓国入門新版)", (Sanseidou, 1992) P16   P35

9. Min KyeongBae, same book P399   P36

10. Tadao Umesao (梅棹忠夫) "Thinking about the Images of Mankind in the 21st Century (二十一世紀の人類像をさぐる)" (Kodansya, 1989) P213-214   P36

11. Ham SeokHeon, same book P29   P37

12. Arch Campbell, *The Christ of the Korean Heart* (Pennsylvania: Christian Literature Crusade, 1954), P.8.

13. Takahiro Suzuki, "What was the reason Korea became a majority Christian country in a short term" : Seirei Christopher University Social Welfare Faculty Journal Vol. 8 (March 2010) P.1-16

14. Choe GilSeong, Anthropology of 'Han' trans. Yuuko Manabe (Hirakawa Press, 1994) P 19

15. Ick Won Kim, *A study of the Korean Church growth in context of Korean national characteristics* (unpublished dissertation, Doctor of Ministry, Pasadena: Fuller Theological Seminary, 1983), P.59.

16. Joo-Young Sohn, Prayer and Church Growth in Korea (unpublished dissertation for Doctorate of Ministry, Pasadena: Fuller Theological Seminary, 1987), P.65.

17. Mayumi Shigematsu, "Shamanism in the country in the late 1970s" eds. Mutsuhiko Shima and Toshio Asakura The Changing of Korean Society - from the field of anthropological research from the 1970s to the 1980s. (Daiichi Shobou 1998). P. 127

18. Peter Seung-Han Kim, A Strategy for Growth and Development for the Andong Presbyterian Church (unpublished thesis, Doctorate of Ministry, Pasadena: Fuller Theological Seminary, 1983).

19. Joo-Young Sohn, op, cit., from p.104

20. Byeon JeChang ed. Running with the Holy Spirit – Witnessing Through Belief. (Ibaraki-Ken, Shobokusya Press 1997) P. 104-113

21. Sundo Kim, The Training of Lay Ministers for Church Growth Through Small Groups in the GwangLim Methodist Church (unpublished dissertation, Doctor of Ministry, Pasadena: Fuller Theological Seminary, 1983), pp. 141-146.

22. Kenji Hidemura, Chapter 8: The Difficulties Between the Pastor and Church Elders – The Conflict of Korean Church A. eds. Ahito Ito, Han GyeongGu, Comparison of the structure of society in Korea and Japan. (Keio Gijuku University Press, 2002) P. 227-240.

23. Research Group F (Yoshihiro Kishi, Shoichi Konda, Takahiro Suzuki, Michio Hamano, and Kaoru Hirose) Group Project "*What made the spread of Christianity not fruitful in Japan*" (Inochino Kotobasya, 2012)

ABOUT THE AUTHOR

Takahiro Suzuki

Born 1942.

ThM. Graduate School of Tokyo Union Theological Semirary

STM Southern Methodist University Faculty of Theology, USA

DMin Western American Baptist Theological University

Worked 40 years as a pastor:

The United Church of Christ in Japan of Higasi Tsurumai Church, Taura Church, Ginza Church, Shoei Church, and America United Methodist Church of Whitney Memorial Methodist Church and others.

Currently Professor at Seirei Christopher University (Hamamatsu City)

Managing Research Group of Independent Missionaries "To the ends of the earth"

http://chinohate.web.fc2.com/

Books written by:

Bible/Belief/Life (High School textbook, compilation. Shinkyo Press 1978)

The work of pastors (Kyobunkan 2002)

Teaching of Christ (Shunjusya 2007)

The translators:

Sulseob Jo was born and raised in South Korea. She graduated from university in South Korea with an undergraduate degree in Chinese characters. She then moved to Japan to study at Nagoya University where she earned a Masters and a PhD in Chinese literature. She is a professor teaching a wide range of subjects from Korean language to Chinese literature as well as Asian culture. She is the author of several books on learning Korean language. She and her husband live in Japan with their two sons.

Allen Williams was born and raised in the United States. He graduated from Murray State University with a Bachelors in Broadcast and a Masters in American Literature. He then earned a PhD while living and working in South Korea. He is the author of several textbooks for English language learning as well as for learning Korean. After spending 6 years in Korea, he moved to Japan where he lives with his wife and two sons and teaches at university.

www.ingramcontent.com/pod-product-compliance
Lightning Source LLC
LaVergne TN
LVHW051057080426
835508LV00019B/1929